South From Corregidor

Lieutenant Commander John Morrill
U.S.N.
and Pete Martin

All rights reserved. No part of this publication may be
reproduced, stored in a retrieval system, or transmitted in any form or by any means, electronic, mechanical,
photocopying or otherwise, without the prior permission of the copyright owner.

© Copyright 2019 by Desert Publishing

desert.books@yahoo.com

For the Men of the U. S. Mine Sweeper *Quail*

INNER SANCTUM BOOKS FOR VICTORY

REPORT FROM TOKYO
by Joseph C. Grew

MISSION TO MOSCOW
by Joseph E. Davies

VICTORY THROUGH AIR POWER
by Major Alexander P. de Seversky

THE INNER SANCTUM EDITION OF
WAR AND PEACE
by Leo Tolstoy

SHOOTING THE RUSSIAN WAR
by Margaret Bourke-White

HOW WAR CAME
by Forrest Davis and Ernest K. Lindley

REPORT ON ENGLAND
by Ralph Ingersoll

THIS IS LONDON
by Edward R. Murrow

ALL OUT
by Samuel Grafton

FOREWORD

THE WAR is teaching us that heroes are likely to be simple men, and self-effacing. When, after much questioning, you get them to discuss their part in it, they do it without vainglory or mock modesty, quietly and matter-of-factly. It is only afterward, when you have had time to think about the stories they tell, that those stories take on epic proportions.

Lieutenant Commander Morrill is like that. He has a quick mind, is pleasant company and more than a little shy. Yet there are times when you see in his face a hint of the qualities which brought him through the fiery furnace of Cavite and the slowly closing steel trap that was Bataan and Corregidor, and in the end carried seventeen men of the mine sweeper *Quail* through thirty-one days in a thirty-six-foot boat navigating Jap-infested seas.

He gives some of the credit for his dramatic and seemingly impossible feat to luck, but most of it to the men who went with him. "I didn't carry them with me," he says; "they carried me."

Obviously, many things must have "carried" them through to safety. Among them: courage, ingenuity and adaptability, tenacity of purpose, and teamwork, especially teamwork.

At the end of one of my sessions of note-taking, one in which Morrill had gone even deeper than usual into stark hardship and peril endured, he said to me with utmost sincerity, "You fellows who write certainly have a hard job.

I don't see how you stand it." I almost went down for the count.

The feeling that exists between Morrill and the seventeen men who went with him must be seen and heard at first hand to be believed. It cannot be put into words. At various times I have tried to sum it up in terms of a father-and-son relationship, of the feeling of brother for brother, of Damon for seventeen Pythiases, but none of these quite does the trick.

When three of his men appeared on the Kate Smith radio hour with Morrill, I talked to them, hoping to unearth further dope to fatten up Morrill's account. I talked to each of the three separately, but invariably, in spite of efforts to get them to talk about themselves, they brought the conversation back to Morrill. The gist of their remarks was, "There is nobody like him—you ought to see him in action when the chips are down—he made us feel like we were all working together—he's a *man*." You could see that all of them were hoping to serve under him again and would drop whatever they happened to be doing if that opportunity ever came.

Morrill is able to put his feeling into practical form. His share of the royalties of this book will be divided eighteen ways on a share-and-share-alike basis.

As *The New York Times* puts it: "It is they—marines, pilots, soldiers, and sailors of the ranks—who tell us more eloquently than all the war speeches what we are fighting for. Because they are there, we all live in the unknown islands of the Pacific. They have become a suburb of all the towns in America."

Morrill is a collaborator's dream, talking.

He has a memory as sensitive as a photographic plate. He

remembered not only the big, dramatic things, but the small, human things that give a story a heartbeat and make it breathe and live. He was conscious of how things smelled, looked, sounded, and felt, as well as where he had been and what he had done.

He is a natural phrasemaker. Pungent, salty words that crackle with the ring of truth come easily to him. Talking to him, I took down four hundred and fifty pages of longhand notes and stuck faithfully to the spirit and mood of those four hundred and fifty pages. But when, as sometimes happened, those notes seemed only the bare bones of a scene or incident, Morrill sat down to his own typewriter and pecked out page after page of further details that put muscle and flesh and blood into the yarn. He has the gift for short, simple, direct sentences that professional writers strive for all of their lives and often never achieve.

If he hadn't been a naval officer he could have been a bang-up writer of action and adventure prose.

Morrill's story is a story of men living and working together in the face of peril.

It is not the story of a one-man show, or even a two- or three-man show. And it is a better and more heartening story thereby.

He was born in Miller, South Dakota, in 1903, was raised in Minneapolis, and was graduated from the Naval Academy in 1924. A brother of his was a naval aviator in the last war.

In June, 1939, he was transferred to the mine sweeper *Quail* as commanding officer. On December 10 of last year the *Quail* was just finishing a Navy Yard overhauling at Cavite in Manila Harbor and testing out its repaired engines when the first wave of Jap planes rocketed overhead.

"We just kept right on testing her," Morrill says, "also our guns."

For this action Morrill received a citation and the Navy Cross.

The citation reads in part as follows: "Lieutenant Commander Morrill, displaying extraordinary courage and determination, proceeded to the dangerous area and towed disabled ships to safety, thereby undoubtedly saving the crews from serious danger and the vessels for further war service."

After the fall of Manila, the *Quail*'s primary function was mine sweeping from Corregidor to seaward. Its secondary function was to act as a watchdog and see to it that no Jap boats sneaked up on the Rock. It had a third unofficial function of its own it called "bird-dogging" Jap planes, which meant trying to catch them over Bataan just as they came up out of a dive after attacking the airfield.

At seven o'clock every morning the Japs sent up a scout plane before beginning its day's strafing and bombing. Morrill and the other mine sweepers gunning for them called this scout plane "Oscar." Each ship got at least one Oscar. After that the Oscars stayed so high the guns couldn't reach them.

Morrill is married to a Philadelphia girl. They have a son, John, aged nine, and a daughter, Jill, six years old. His wife was at Pearl Harbor on the fateful morning of December 7. She was back in Philadelphia when she received a telegram dated May 9: REGRET TO ADVISE YOU THAT PENDING FURTHER INFORMATION YOUR HUSBAND IS MISSING. On June 16 she got a radiogram from Australia: HOW AND WHERE ARE YOU. I AM WELL. It was signed "Jack."

PETE MARTIN

CONTENTS

	Foreword	vii
1.	Mine Sweeping Around Bataan	1
2.	The Tunnel in the Rock	17
3.	Sandbags and Fox Holes	32
4.	Escape from Caballo	48
5.	Out to Sea	74
6.	Hide-and-Seek	83
7.	Helping Hands	100
8.	Plan of Action	122
9.	Dodging the Red-balls	142
10.	Action off Longaskagawayan Point	166
11.	Through the Indies	182
12.	Engine Trouble	206
13.	The Last Lap	224
	Epilogue	247

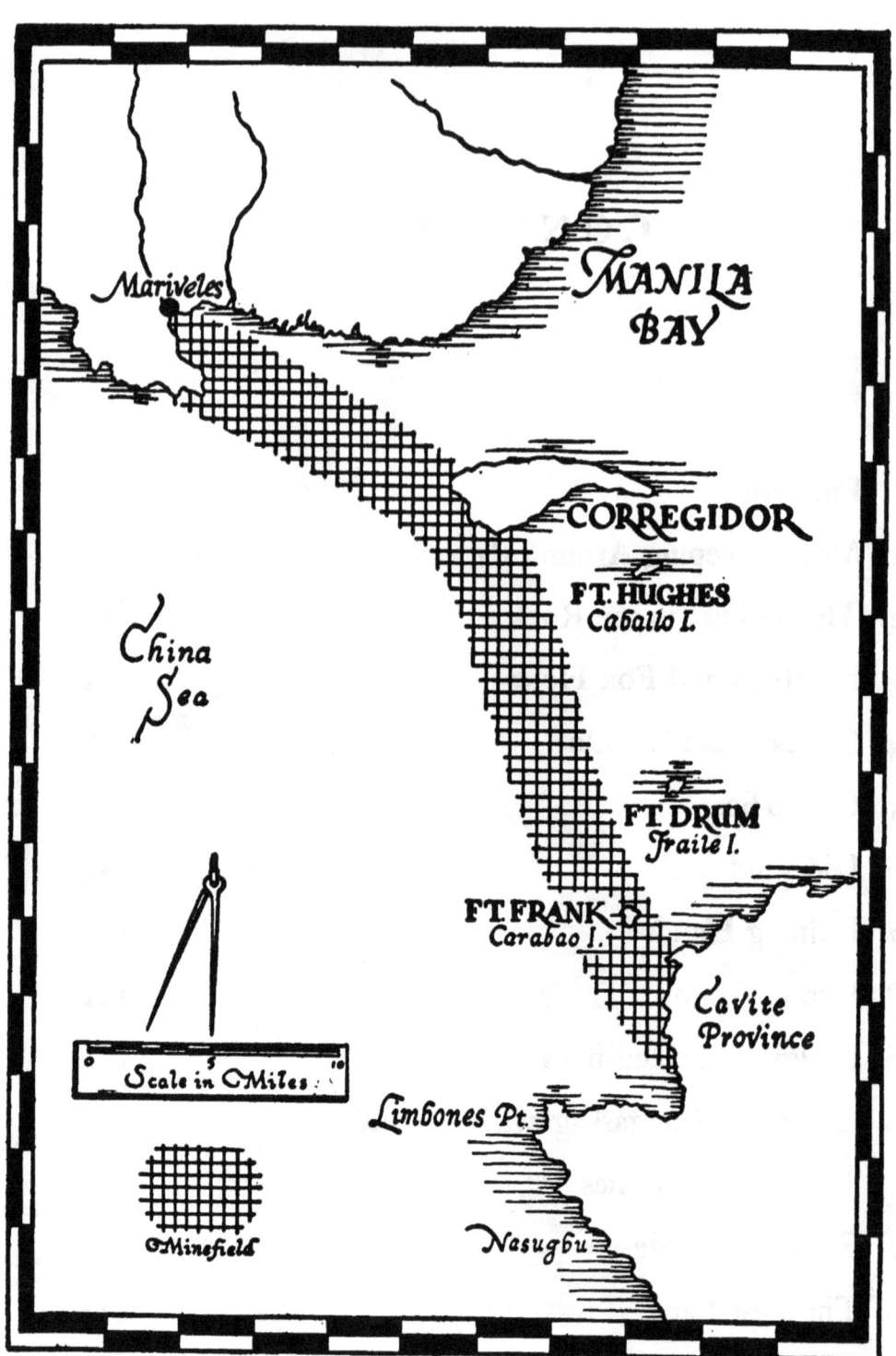

1

Mine Sweeping Around Bataan

BATAAN DIED protesting, hating the business of dying. A handful of its guns complained about it bitterly to the end. We on the mine sweeper *Quail* had wondered how long it could last. As many as a hundred and eighty-five Jap bombers had worked the place over from sunrise to sunset and all through the nights, without any letup during which a man could close his eyes, or leave his fox hole to choke down skimpy rations of salmon and rice. We were beginning to find out that bravery is often a matter of having enough vitamins.

Now that the Japs were coming through they were coming through a junk heap—there weren't any front lines. The defense areas had been erased by the very effective process of grinding them into powdered rubble. Some of our men who managed to get away to Corregidor told me that they found Jap troops as many as six miles in their rear when the end came.

With their planes gone, our aviators and mechanics at Cab Cabin tried their hand at being ground troops. They were dishing it out with everything they could get hold of, but it wasn't enough to prolong the agony. Bataan was finished.

Before it was over we were to see Corregidor die too, and Fort Drum and Fort Hughes. Eighteen of us were to be the last ones to get away after the white flags had gone up and our men in the tunnels had been lined up and disarmed by their own officers, ready for the Japs to take over—but not being fortunetellers we couldn't tell it would be like that.

A soldier or sailor isn't told what goes on around him. Headquarters doesn't broadcast a play-by-play description of the game; it's too huge, confused, and complex. A man has to try to interpret things for himself, and that is what we tried to do. For weeks we had had our own scouts out gathering information. Whenever we sent a working party over to Sisilman Cove or Mariveles to draw out drums of Diesel oil for our boats, we sent along one or more extra men or an officer who circulated around Bataan, picked up what information he could during the day, and returned at night with the working party bringing back the oil. We knew the effect the starvation rations were having on our soldiers. We knew they were begging their officers to let them make a suicidal attempt to break through the Jap lines and reach the food in the provinces beyond. Sometimes we sent over little donations of our own ship's food supply, but it was a very small drop in a very large bucket. Bataan was a heartbreaking place. The sailors hated to go over there, but we needed to know not only if it was going to fall but also how and, as nearly as possible, when.

We dug up every drum of Diesel oil we could find hidden away in the brush on the hillsides. We begged every

Mine Sweeping Around Bataan

round of ammunition the *Canopus* could spare us from her submarine stock. The *Canopus* was an old pre-World War German cargo boat. The Navy had taken her over and made her into a submarine tender for duty on the Asiatic station. We carefully husbanded our own food supply; but there was little or no oil for the ship's boilers. We had loaded our reserve oil supply on a barge, then flooded it and sunk it in Sisilman Cove. We kept an anxious eye on that barge. It held scarcely enough for the hungry boilers of one ship, and nine ships needed it, besides the auxiliary power plants in the forts. And we knew we would have to make a break while we still had fuel to fire our boilers if we were ever to get those ships out of the trap they were in.

We figured that when Bataan fell we'd slug our way out somehow past the ever-tightening blockade of Jap destroyers around Corregidor. It was a one-to-twenty bet but it was a chance we were willing to take. Our three small mine sweepers together hardly equaled one Jap destroyer in fire power, but on the *Quail* we made up our minds we were going to have a fling at it anyhow, and the captains and crews of the mine sweepers *Tanager* and *Finch* were as eager to make the attempt as we.

But when the zero hour came we couldn't go. We had to stay and sweep a new channel through our own mine field so that a blockade-running sub or a rescue expedition could get through to Corregidor. Before the end, a sub did use the channel we made, but the relief expedition sailed only in our minds.

A heavyhearted trio of mine-sweeper skippers gathered in the wardroom of the *Quail* the morning Bataan fell, to talk over the mine-sweeping job that had been given us. Besides myself there were Adolph Roth, the skipper of the *Tanager*, and Davison, skipper of the *Finch*. Roth was a short, youngish, ruddy man who had just recently been given command of the *Tanager*, relieving the division commander. He had been exec officer on the *Childs* but was young for his present berth. Davison was tall, stringy, and sandy-haired. He was about Roth's age. As a matter of fact, they were both eight or nine years younger than I and since I'd had two years' mine-sweeping experience and they had had their jobs only a few months, they naturally looked to me to find the answers to the questions the situation was putting up to us. We had seen the violent explosions on Bataan the night before. Fires had licked around the ammunition dumps and smoke covered the hills. Through it we could see tongues of flame and rocks as big as boxcars hurtling upward. Over toward Mariveles Bay our gas tanks were burning, and fire balls rose from them to spread into huge, terrifying mushrooms. One large explosion at Mariveles tore the top of a small mountain loose, and fragments as big as houses splattered over Mariveles Harbor and the boats evacuating men from Bataan. When the water spouts sank back down again some of the boats were gone.

The most unforgettable sight of all was the groups of men standing on the south Bataan shore in the early half-light of morning, beckoning and signaling with flashlights for help. The gunboats *Mindanao*, *Luzon*, and *Oahu* were over there picking them up as fast as they could. How many they ferried across to Corregidor we never knew, but eventually Corregidor could hold no more.

Now we had to leave to its fate our oil supply sunk in

Sisilman Cove. We had our work mapped out for us. A mine field is usually swept working carefully from its edges in—this one was made up of live mines set to go off on contact and not when a push button on shore exploded them electrically. Ordinarily in picking them up we used a long sweep wire with little sharp knives set into its trailing loop. The mines would drift down into the dangling half circle until they hit the knives, which faced both ways so that no matter which way the mine came into the trap, if their cables weren't cut by one knife they would be sliced in two by another. We would take our ships along the edge of the field, working on it from off to one side in safe water. But this wasn't an ordinary assignment. We wouldn't be picking up a mine field. We were slicing a path straight through it.

The time to lick a problem like that, we knew, was before you started, and not after half a ton of TNT slammed you into the middle of next week. To take the *Quail* or any other mine sweeper directly across the field would have meant certain destruction. The answer we came up with was to make a series of preliminary sweeps with shallow draft boats. We could use Manila rope instead of sweep wire and tow the mines into deep water and sink them.

Feverishly we plotted the endless details of the job. Every few minutes word came down from the *Quail*'s bridge and each report was more alarming. The Japs were coming down the Bataan peninsula, bringing their artillery with them. Their planes were using our Bataan airfield. Davison and Roth, the skippers of the *Tanager* and *Finch*, were restless and anxious to return to their own ships. But our mine-sweeping job took precedence over everything else and had to be started as soon as humanly possible. We sent out orders to light off our dead boilers and went on planning.

Late morning wore on to early afternoon. Lunch was no problem as we had been on two meals a day for a long time. At last, when we were completing the final details, the general-alarm howler brought us out of it with a jolt. Davison and Roth made a dive through the door toward their boats waiting alongside. I went through the other door and raced up the ladder to the bridge.

The flaming hell that was Bataan had caught up with us. The Japs had set up artillery batteries all along the Bataan shore. Over to the westward they had scored a hit on one of our tugs, the *Keswick*, and she was on fire. It was two giant steps back over to the engine-room voice tube, but I made it in one. The engineers didn't have to be called. They must have had their ears glued to the tubes, waiting for the order they knew would come, and were already boosting the steam pressure up past the pace-time safety maximum.

Our boilers carried 150 pounds normally and were tested for a hundred per cent overload, but that day we worked up to 210 or 215 pounds before we were through. Normally the transition from lying with dead boilers, conserving fuel oil, to a condition of more than full power would be an operation of many hours. It was a much shorter time than that with us. How much shorter I won't say. It might give our bureau of engineering heart failure.

Counting from Cab Cabin westward along the south shore there were twenty-odd Jap batteries and more farther inland on the Bataan slopes. It was sickening to look at the *Keswick*. Her crew were huddled forward helplessly, and the Jap batteries were hosing shells into them. The Japs must have got a kick out of it and decided they wanted more of the same, for they decided to try for our bigger ships. This time they bit off a much bigger mouthful. The ships were all moving now, just as we were, with the *Mindanao* leading the attack. No orders were given, nor was there time for any. Gathering speed as she went, the *Mindanao* slid along the coastline, zigzagging. Holding her fire until she reached a position between the Jap batteries and the *Keswick*, she opened up and pounded the daylights out of those batteries. It seemed utter recklessness, and we held our breath for her. We should have known it was a waste of time to worry about her skipper, McCracken. In no time at all he blew the batteries all to hell and maneuvered his ship alongside the *Keswick* to rescue her crew.

It was a maneuver which called for fearlessness, and McCracken did it without thinking, as naturally as he would blink an eye. He rated a decoration for it, but time worked against him and the records of his exploit were destroyed when Corregidor fell.

He was a small, dark Scotch-American, and action like this was old stuff to him. Not long before, he had chased a Jap boat all the way back to Cavite. The Jap shore guns opened up on him with ten or twelve six-inchers. McCracken stayed with them, dishing it out with his two little three-inchers. We could see the fur flying through our glasses from Corregidor. Annoyed by his impudence, the Japs sent a six-plane formation out to slap him down. But McCracken kept in there slugging away with them, even with a double battle on his hands.

Our headquarters got wind of what was going on and by radio ordered him back. Being thus interrupted and deprived of Japs, he felt very lonely and came back the long way, via Manila, looking for company. Several hours later, after many plaintive, "What are you doing now, McCracken?" calls from H.Q., he steamed back and anchored.

He hadn't been able to get as close to Manila as he wanted. There had been too many sunken hulks in the way. But he had found and chased three Jap launches, sinking one. In the process he had also found out where the Jap Manila batteries were located, which would have been a useful thing to know if long-expected reinforcements had ever come.

But this was a tougher day altogether, and after it was over the *Mindanao* was marooned in South Harbor. She was badly hurt. A shell had landed in her engine room and messed things up so she never got over it. McCracken kept her afloat by will power and constant pumping, and by the time she foundered he had stripped her of everything useful and had got her guns and supplies off. Finally she turned over and sank, escaping air making a snoring noise in her funnels like a tired Irish-biddy scrubwoman rolling over in bed. When that happened the *Mindanao*'s men were turned over to the Army, and McCracken was made assistant to the Commandant at Navy Headquarters tunnel on the Rock.

But now we didn't watch McCracken any more. We were busy picking out our own targets. The *Pigeon*, the other mine sweepers, and the gunboats were hogging the show along the south shore, so we moved along to the northeast, toward the Jap batteries at Cab Cabin. It was made up of four fieldpieces, and they opened up on us with a wild salvo over our heads. That gave us their location, which was what we wanted.

The *Quail* was a comparatively small ship—she was built to be an 850-tonner and was 185 feet long, but with the modernization they had given her and with her new armor plate she weighed 1250 tons.

On small ships you have to double up on jobs, and Taylor was our gunnery officer, spotter, battery-control officer, and antiaircraft-control man. Taylor had a bad leg and foot, although he tried to play down his affliction. He had spent a lot of time in the hospital trying to lick the tropical disease which was threatening to cripple him, but the doctors in the tunnel hospital had given up. He kept chafing at restraint and wanting to get back on board on active duty, and the hell with his ailing prop. He was a pale, rather delicate type, dark, and small-boned, four or five inches taller than myself—not that that made him a giant, for I'm no man mountain—and he was the intense, worrying kind whose nervous energy stores up and breaks out in spurts and jets when the pressure is on. Despite his intensity he had a pleasing manner, and my wife says he is handsome.

He stood on the forward part of the bridge, wearing a telephone headset. Near his right hand were the controls for giving commence- and cease-firing orders to our eight groups of fifty-caliber antiaircraft machine guns. His earphones were split. One ear was connected with the three-inch gun that was firing against the Japs' shore battery; the other ear was connected with the three-inch gun that was to keep dive bombers off our tail.

You can't hear a shout during a battle no matter how loudly you yell, so I took a position between Taylor and our helmsman. The motions I made with my arm told the helmsman which way to throw the rudder and the engine-room speed indicators. A thump on Taylor's back attracted his attention so that he could see me pointing out a new target. Sometimes I thumped him too hard; and he turned around ready to fight me and the Japs too.

The Jap battery at Cab Cabin was duck soup. Taylor's first shot missed it by fifty yards. His second was a bull's-eye and brought up flying parts of gun-carriage wheels and Jap arms and legs. We gave them four or five more shots to make sure, then looked around for more targets. They weren't easy to find. The *Pigeon* and the other ships were laying them out right and left. We decided to have a try for some of the batteries farther away up on the hills, although to do it we would have to run in closer to get within range. But we never got around to it, for just then we got a cease-firing radio message from our headquarters.

We found out later that while our shells were pounding the shore, General King was over there negotiating Bataan's surrender with the Japs and he and his party were in our line of fire.

As it turned out, we had stirred up a hornets' nest and we couldn't have given the shore batteries much more attention anyhow. The Jap army must have put in a hurry call for their air force to help them out, for over it came, all of it. Before that, they had shown only a casual interest in our ships, mostly trying to pick off lame ducks who got separated from the rest, such as a mine sweeper at work. But now they were after us, hell-bent for election, and they weren't fooling.

Dive bombers came over in threes. Each group tried to single out one of our ships and concentrate on it, but we had an answer to that. Back in January the Japs had nearly knocked off the *Perry* by concentrating on it all of one afternoon. We made up our minds not to let them do that now and kept our ships in tight triangles with each side of the triangle about a thousand yards long. They couldn't pick out a ship and go for it without catching it three ways at once from us, and the triangle allowed them so little air room their groups of threes got in each other's way.

Even with the triangle, each of our ships watched every wiggle those planes made. Just before a dive bomber goes into a dive it noses up and pulls into a sort of stall. When that time comes you must be making all the speed your boilers will give you, even if you have to hang a weight on the safety valve to hold it down. Above all, you must be turning. We used circles and figure eights for dive bombers, and they had to be tight, rapid circles because a dive bomber and his bombs come down fast.

The Japs tried their best to get on our tails, where our gunfire was weakest, but they couldn't solve the triangle setup.

Still, it was no Sunday-school picnic for us. Taylor had both his three-inch guns working as A.A. now, and it took split-second timing to do it right. The gun crews shucked clothes until they were stripped to the waist, and sweat ran rivers down the hollows between their shoulder blades. They loaded the stuff into the gun breeches for hours without a break. When a loader was so pooped he couldn't wiggle a finger he changed off with a pointer or trainer, making the change quickly so that the rhythm of firing wouldn't be interrupted even for a second.

This was a different day from any that had gone before. In the past one or two dive-bombing attacks on us had been a day's work for the Japs. Most of the bombing had been of the high-altitude, heavy, flat type. There is as much difference between the flats and the dive bombers as between a game of croquet and a free-for-all. The high flats are slow-moving, big crates, easy to see and easy to dodge. Sometimes when we got home on a heavy flat with a three-inch shell it just disappeared. One minute the plane would be sitting above us, big and arrogant-looking. The next instant there'd be the puff of our shell bursting, and almost immediately his fuel tank would blow up. A narrow column of smoke moving down and some black pieces of what looked like burned paper falling lazily would be all there was left of him. Then sometimes when we got home with a surprise package of shrapnel we couldn't tell right away whether we had connected or not. Maybe he'd start to lose altitude and slip down on a long flat zoom until he piled up in a wave; or perhaps he wobbled over the hills out of sight. If we were lucky, the lookouts high on the Rock would send us word we'd finished him.

When you're working on the flats like that there is time for wisecracks and kidding. The gun crews used to squint through their sights and start cussing before the Japs were within range. Gun Two would call over, "Come on, Gun One, let's get those yellow bastards." Gun Two always seemed to be luckier. Sometimes when the gun-one pointer squeezed his trigger he got a misfire. When that happened the port gun crew would look over again with mock sympathy as if appalled by such incompetence. An occasional shell was bound to be a dud because the stuff issued to us was old and had deteriorated, but it didn't console the starboard crew. Their gun captain danced with rage. "If this damn thing don't go off this time," he'd yell, "I'm going to throw the —— gun at 'em."

A week before, the port crew had threatened to paint "Miss Misfire" on the starboard gun barrel but they hadn't done it. There would have been a riot if they had.

In the past when we brought down a Jap plane, the men topside used to let out a yip that sounded all over the ship, but not today. Things were happening too fast.

The sun was a burning, blistering, white-hot disk. Hess and Haley, the bos'n's mates, were barefooted. The deck plates would have cooked an ordinary foot, but a bos'n's soles get tough after a while and he builds up an extra protection of callus, like retreading a tire. Even so, they couldn't stand it very long at a time. They lifted first one foot and then the other and rubbed the heat out slowly against their other leg. The place where the gun crews worked was littered with empty shell cases, and the men suffered skin burns from the empties banging against their shins.

These things I saw only in flashes; most of the time I had my glasses nailed on targets, waiting for that telltale stall and flip-over.

The Jap dive bombers were coming in fast now. They came in groups of threes. Three over us and three over the gunboats. Each group would make two runs, one complete run to release each of their two bombs. In all there were somewhere in the neighborhood of fifty dive bombers working over that area, taking their turns in trios. Taylor had a hard time getting his gun crews and machine gunners to make the break away from one target in time to meet the next one, but it had to be done. If we failed to put up a barrage in front of any one of those red-balls he'd be right down on us, plane, bomb and all.

We began to long for dusk to put a stop to it. Since we were steaming at full power our oil was falling away fast, and we couldn't have mourned each drop of it more if it had been our life's blood heating our boilers. Toward sunset a last group of Jap planes began to concentrate on the gunboats, and since the gunboats were not as well armed as we were we moved our triangle over toward them. But they didn't get the gunboats. They didn't get a single ship that day. We didn't know what our score was. You don't even have time to watch a plane fall in a melee like that. It's always "the next one" you've got to watch. The Army, keeping count over on Corregidor, gave us credit for dunking a highly satisfactory number in the bay, but we figured the Army was stretching things a little bit in our favor to cheer us up. They chalked up six or eight for us, but such figures are unreliable. We'd learned to be skeptical of all such reports and of our own guesses, too. You don't really feel satisfied that you've knocked off one unless you've seen it fall yourself.

After sunset we went in and anchored the *Quail* at the

end of the new channel we had been told to sweep. When our stomachs quit churning inside of us we broke out our coffee percolators and had coffee and then, a little later, dinner.

I've noticed that right after an action like that nobody talks. Maybe they are punchy. Maybe they are emotionally exhausted. I remember when I was a kid and went to see *All Quiet on the Western Front* I couldn't talk to anybody for two hours afterward. Going through an *All Quiet* yourself is ten times as shattering an experience. After a while our breath began to come back, and the storage tanks where we kept our endurance began to fill up again. But we didn't say a word, except for orders, until we'd finished our evening meal.

We let our boiler fires die out to save fuel oil, but the little we had left was hardly worth saving. It made the crew miserable to have the ship cold and dead like that. They knew as well as I did that only movement, and fast movement, could save a ship under attack.

In the evening a group of the *Quail*'s officers and crew gathered on the bridge to talk things over. We had made a habit of doing that after a bad day. The thing weighing on our minds was Corregidor. We wondered how long it could last now that Bataan was gone. We knew that if we lost the *Quail* we'd all be sent ashore to help the Army. A few of our men and a lot of the gunboats' crews had already been drafted for that purpose. Since our fate was bound up with the Rock, we went into a kind of question-and-answer game.

Question: "Captain, why can't we slug our way out past those Jap destroyers tonight?"

Answer: "You know we can't. We've got to sweep this blasted new channel through our mine field."

Question: "Captain, if Corregidor surrenders, will we have to surrender too?"

Answer: "Hell, no. If we've still got the ship we'll steam out of here until we run out of oil, and then take to the hills. The final answer is the boats. Since we haven't got enough oil to get anywhere, the Commandant will probably want the ship scuttled to keep it from falling into Jap hands. From now on, no matter what else you do, keep the boats full of Diesel oil and supplies. All the boats. We'll need them all, and more too, if we're going to get all hands out. And another thing, if we all get sent ashore, don't get lost—stick close, and if you are sent on outpost duty, leave word where I can find you. Corregidor's a big place and there are about thirteen thousand men over there."

This question-and-answer game was prophetic. We were sent ashore the next day and, except for odd moments thereafter, we lived on the ship only at night and then merely a skeleton crew of us.

2

The Tunnel in the Rock

For three days and nights we worked dismounting the *Quail*'s guns and transporting them over to Corregidor. The Army Ordnance and the marines built mounts for them, and the sailors who had served them on shipboard went ashore to man them or teach somebody else how to do it.

Those of the crew who were left on board tried to cut the channel at night and sleep in the tunnel by day. We had spent so much of our time blacked out we had learned to live and work in darkness. Many of the sailors were so used to not seeing what their hands were doing they could handle a repair job by feel. They had literally trained themselves to see with their fingers.

Being under special orders, I had divided my crew into halves and used part of them on this work and the other part on the mine-sweeping chore. We lost the mine sweeper *Finch* on the eleventh of April, and the Commandant decided to disarm the others while we still had something to disarm.

On the eleventh we had anchored in such fashion that

we served as a marker at the end of the channel we were sweeping. The *Tanager*, having no definite place to berth, chose the middle of South Harbor. The *Finch* picked out a spot close up against the sheer cliff of Caballo Island, where there was deep water within a stone's throw of land. She figured that dive bombers couldn't get at her there because they couldn't zoom down over Caballo. But on that same day heavy bombers gave Caballo a hell of a going over and in doing so some of the bombs spilled over the cliff and wrecked the *Finch*. When she sank she lay up against the island, all ripped apart.

We sent two thirds of our machine guns ashore but were allowed to keep our three-inch guns. When the unloading was done, two thirds of the men who had been doing it were ordered to stay on Corregidor at the disposal of the Army and help form a final defense man-power reserve.

Just before dawn every morning we went over to the Rock to make a full report of the progress we had made during the night.

Then I'd either try to sleep in the tunnel or climb up high on the rocks of Malinta Hill, where the marines had machine-gun dugouts. The thing I remember most vividly about them is the way they sighted along the barrels of their machine guns, figuring how many Japs they could mow down with the ammunition they had. They were very happy with the heavy machine guns we sent them from the ship, only they were a little rough in handling them. We had to lend them gunners' mates to teach them about the upkeep of the intricate parts.

A little farther down Malinta Hill there were emplace-

The Tunnel in the Rock

ments with seventy-five-millimeter beach-defense guns, manned by marines and serviced by soldiers commanded by Lieutenant Crotty. It was a good fighting team and held a key position overlooking Monkey Point. Later on, when it was wiped out by artillery fire and the last submarine brought no replacement guns for it, we knew Corregidor was going to fall.

Whenever I could, I let my men sleep on the *Quail*. I had found out that after two or three days in the tunnel they got a disease which, for want of a better word, I called "tunnelitis." Feeling safe for the moment and huddling in tight sweaty groups with other men who felt temporarily safe, they let down their guards mentally. I sent brave men into the place, and after they had been exposed to whatever evil thing the tunnel did to them, they came back to the ship and sat and shivered on her decks, their nerves jangling at finding themselves out in the open again, with no rock roof over them.

I've read a lot about the Army tunnel but I haven't read much about the hole bored in the rock the Navy lived in. Because of the long dry spell and Jap high explosives, the dust was so thick in it, it was almost impossible to breathe. You sat in it and gasped for air. Flies were all over the place, little black ones that bit like mosquitoes. When you couldn't stand it any longer, you went outside, even during heavy shellfire, to fill your lungs with deep inhalations of something untainted and dust-free. A lot of men were killed just trying to breathe. Our latrine was a makeshift wooden affair with a shed roof over it, approximately fifty yards outside the tunnel. About the middle of April a bomb landed a few yards away from it. One of our men was in it, occupying one of its lowly thrones, and when the dust settled we could see him sitting there still alive, but frozen into a horrified statue, with debris draped around his neck. He was shell-shocked and dazed and suffered from concussion but was unhurt. Someone ran out and grabbed him and dragged him back into the tunnel, and it was hours before he realized what had happened or before anyone felt like laughing.

The piping for the tunnel sewage was impromptu, and the humidity made the place like a Turkish bath. The walls were always sweating and damp. The average temperature inside was around 98°. When a bomb landed at the tunnel mouth, the concussion blew dust and trash right through the place from one end to the other. There was a makeshift ventilating system, but its main function was to pump dust-fouled air into an already dust-fouled place.

Corregidor had supplies for a protracted siege, but, not knowing how long a session we were in for, we were put on one-third rations after Bataan fell. Up to that time my crew on the *Quail* had made out better than the Bataan troops. But afterward, we turned our chow into the common pool and began to live on canned salmon and rice, twice a day. Even after that, we were still in better shape than most of the others, because our pharmacist's mate had been farsighted enough to lay in a store of vitamin pills before the war, and we had been throwing them into the crew like popcorn whenever we got a chance.

During the next few weeks, the Japs perfected their plan of controlled fire. They would put their guns on one spot on Corregidor until they had the range exactly. Then they wouldn't use those particular guns any more until the final assault. They did this again and again, so that when the last attack broke they must have had from three to four hundred guns trained on the Rock's vital spots. Also, by keeping their guns quiet after they had located their final targets, they could avoid counterfire.

During this process the Rock's twelve-inch guns were hit over and over again by direct hits from six-inch guns, but each time what was left of the gun crews picked themselves up to find that, aside from minor damage to the breech blocks, they could keep on firing a little longer. Gradually these guns were put out of action, until by the fifth of May there were only about two big guns still left on Corregidor and one on Caballo. The beach-defense guns, which were our main protection against barge-borne Jap landing parties, were used up one by one and abandoned. The Jap routine was one of creeping attrition. Our ships went the same way—one by one and little by little. Bombs got some of them, but most of the real knockout punches came in the form of shells from Cavite. There wasn't much we could do about it, since most of our ships were empty of oil.

To save fuel we didn't move the *Quail* during the day and used what oil we could spare to shift her out to the mine field at night. Our original idea had been to do our mine sweeping by day as well as by night, but we soon gave it up. On April 11, the *Quail* suffered three hits. It occurred to us then, as it should have before, that if the Japs could see us well enough to hit us, they could also see us well enough to figure out what we were doing over at the edge of the mine field. After that, we worked only at night, sweeping a channel four hundred feet wide. By

May 3, we were ready to start widening it out to six hundred feet. That morning, however, the Commandant told me to have my men take a rest that night. We were in the groove now as far as that work was concerned and had almost grown to count on it as something regular and dependable in a confused and chaotic world. I was taken aback at his order and asked "why."

"Turn in and take a sleep," the Commandant said. "I'll tell you why later."

I grabbed my sleep and went back prick-eared for the "why." By that time he was ready to tell me. A sub was coming in to evacuate a group of nurses and officers from Corregidor, and the Commandant wanted me to pilot a boat through the channel we had swept through the mine field and ferry the group who were going out to the sub. He gave me the time and location and impressed upon me the need for secrecy about the undertaking. The thing was very hush-hush. The officers and nurses were given only one hour to pack up and get ready to go.

After sunset, my passengers collected on the South Harbor Dock. The nurses wore khaki pants and shirts and dark-blue capes. They were calm and cool and talked very little. You don't feel like talking much when you're leaving behind you people you've known and worked with and grown close to, through common suffering, for a long time.

Thirteen nurses, sixteen officers, and one civilian and his wife herded into the little pilot steamer assigned to the job. Under my guidance, the steamer captain, a young ensign, picked his way gingerly through the hole we had bored through the mines.

The Tunnel in the Rock

Once we were through the opening, I told the passengers about it, because I knew they were on edge and that was one worry I could relieve them of at least. Then we lay to, to wait for our pig-boat date to show up. Presently she loomed up through the murk, looking bigger than a cruiser. She was blowing the top off her main ballast tanks, like a steel-plated whale coming up for air, and she lay low in the water, with her decks barely awash.

I climbed up on top of the pilot boat's deckhouse, where I was on a level with the conning tower, and while our passengers were being transferred, the sub's skipper and I had a chat. He turned out to be a Lieutenant Dempsey.

I called out "Hello-o-o" to him, and he asked, "Who's that?"

"Morrill," I said.

I didn't know Dempsey, but apparently he knew me or had heard something about my having been a sub skipper like himself, and wondered why I was there.

"I'm just working here," I told him. "What did you bring us?"

"We didn't bring much," he said apologetically. "The crew took up a collection and we've got some cigarettes and candy for your men. We've been busy. We haven't seen daylight for four weeks but we got a Jap flat-top—handed her one in the bellyband and touched off her magazine—and we got a couple of transports too."

It was exciting news, but there were things we needed even more urgently than good news.

"Did you bring us any guns?" I asked, and he shook his head regretfully.

It had been a forlorn hope. Still I had to ask him. We

were getting down to peashooters. We had one Navy antiaircraft gun on Malinta Hill which had been removed from the *Houston* before she left Cavite. Practically singlehanded, this gun had shooed the Jap dive bombers away from Corregidor and the ships until about a week before, when the Japs had planted a shell squarely on the Navy gun mount and wiped it out.

Dempsey looked around into the night and asked curiously, "Don't they ever do any shooting around here? I thought you were having a war."

It was a natural enough question. By some freak of luck he had surfaced during the first two hours in weeks when there wasn't a lot of heavy stuff going off and the air crack-cracking with shells and the crump-p-p of bombs. I explained to him about his good fortune. Then I tried to sketch the Jap patrol lines out for him between Olongago and Fortune Island and the patrol between Fortune Island and Nasugbu and told him how we were hemmed in by a complete circle of ships. Meantime the sub's men were shuttling our passengers down the sub hatches and showing the officers and nurses where to put the ten pounds of clothing they had been allowed. The sub crew gave our crew the cigarettes and candy, and we said good-by and good luck to each other. Ten minutes later we were nearing the channel entrance in the mine field, homeward bound.

The lone civilian who had been given permission to get out to tell his wife good-by was standing looking over the rail, his eyes straining back through the night toward the spot where the sub had vanished into the darkness. I tried to cheer him up, but he was beyond cheering.

"The hardest thing I ever did in my life," he said, "was

to climb up that conning-tower ladder and leave her down there."

At the last minute his wife hadn't wanted to go, and her arms had to be removed from his neck by force.

Just as we entered the channel, the Japs opened up on Corregidor for the first time with their full-dress-rehearsal barrage, to see how well all those guns they had been carefully spotting for three weeks would do. Corregidor was immediately transformed from a towering shape shouldering up into the night into a rock of leaping, flickering fire. It was like a mammoth Fourth-of-July set piece going off. Shells were puncturing the night close to us on all sides. The Japs scored a hit on one of the largest magazines on Fort Mills, and it erupted like a volcano. A roll of flame rolled right down Government Ravine, a steep gorge thickly inhabited by sailors sent ashore from the *Canopus*.

The young ensign of the pilot boat made a gulping noise in his throat. "There go a lot of our boys," he said thickly.

Horror and the crushing sense of the enemy's overwhelming fire power, to which we had no adequate return, pushed down on us like a heavy weight.

We were supposed to anchor at South Dock, but South Dock was almost hidden by shell bursts and leaping spouts of flame. I remember I said, "Dempsey knows *now* whether or not they do any shooting around here. He can hear it out there even if he's submerged."

We decided to take the boat over and tie her up to the stern of the *Quail* and wait to see what happened.

"If this keeps up," the ensign said, "there won't be any Corregidor to go back to."

We hailed the *Quail*, but even where she lay, shells were

splashing around and bursting fragments were banging against steel plates in the dark, racketing a boiler-factory refrain. I knew the little pilot boat didn't have splinter protection, so I took everybody off her and put them on the *Quail*'s gun deck. Three hours later, as suddenly as it began, the barrage stopped, and I sent the little boat to its regular anchorage.

Dempsey's sub was the last one to get through.

During the latter part of January and the first part of February it had been still possible for supply ships to run the Jap blockade by coming up from Cebu at high speed, making the trip entirely by night except for the last few hours. When they arrived off the Lubang Island group about daylight, our lookouts, three hundred feet up on top of Corregidor, would see them and we'd send out one or more PT boats to escort them in.

But after the fall of Singapore, the Japs gave the Philippines more attention with their dive bombers and warships. They bombed Mindanao and picked off our supply ships just off the Lubang Islands, where some of them sank before the agonized eyes of our lookouts peering helplessly through their binoculars.

After that, when we were mine sweeping at night and when we were holed up during the day, we could see and hear dive bombers dropping loads of eggs over Bataan for more than two weeks after its fall. It was mute evidence that large or small groups of our men had somehow escaped the holocaust and had taken to the hills, where they were being hunted down. This was particularly true of the western hills of the peninsula overlooking the west coast, where our Philippine scouts had been stationed.

The Tunnel in the Rock

The dive bombers came so close we could actually see them thumb their noses at us, which was a trick I hadn't realized the Japs knew. There was, however, another trick that belonged peculiarly to them. For months bodies had been floating past us in the water, some of them our marines, some of them soldiers, but most of them Filipinos, with their arms tied behind them and their legs tied together too. These bodies had all been literally cut to pieces by bayonet stabs.

When you've seen such things with your own eyes, your feeling is a deep conviction that you aren't fighting men but animals with men's bodies and dressed in men's clothes, but with strange, slimy jungle growths where their brains ought to be. My own feelings about them hardened into an intense desire to kill them and a stinging regret I couldn't kill more. From what my men said in my hearing, they felt the same way, except that many of them had dedicated themselves more intensively to the idea than I had, if that were possible.

The Filipinos felt even more strongly about it than we did. In the early days of the war we were talking one day in the *Quail's* wardroom about the possibility of capturing Japs. My executive officer and I jokingly promised our Filipino mess boys they could have our first prisoners.

Much later a Jap aviator had his plane shot out from under him and parachuted into the water just off Corregidor. Only Jap officers had parachutes. The common or everyday Jap pilot was supposed to die if he lost his plane. We sent a boat out to pick that Jap up if possible, and while the boat was away, the mess boys sidled up to Lee, the executive officer, and myself and asked, "Mr. Lee, can we have him?"

Lee had forgotten the kidding in the wardroom by this time and asked, "What are you talking about?"

"You and the Captain promised us we could have the first prisoner," they said.

Lee noticed they were holding their hands behind their backs in a peculiar fashion and asked them what they were concealing. Eyes glistening, they brought out two long, sharp carving knifes. Fortunately, we didn't pick that Jap up. He was gone when our boat reached the spot where he was last seen, thereby saving Lee and me from long explanations as to why we couldn't carry out our promise.

You couldn't be too careful about those Jap pilots.

Earlier in the winter they had come flying in an American plane at our boats tied up in the harbor and had bombed the hell out of us before we snapped out of our surprise at seeing one of our own crates with our own silhouette and our own markings on it doing unpleasant things to us. It was an old 1936 army training job which probably had been sold to the Japs in the trusting days when we sent them scrap iron and oil and other items to help them get ready for Pearl Harbor. But we got that particular one and arranged for him to take a long, deep sleep on the Cavite shore. From then on we made it a standing rule that if any plane, no matter what it seemed to be, came at us head on and persisted in coming at us, we'd throw up a burst or two of A.A. in front of him to warn him away, and if he acted bullheaded about it we really got down to business.

Notwithstanding, we looked up one day to see a little

Philippine training plane heading in our direction. We tried him out with a burst in front. He swerved and flipped his wings but kept right on coming. The Jap we had piled up on Cavite had flipped his wings too, so that didn't mean anything to us. Next we nudged this trainer craft with three-inch stuff and bolstered that up with fifty-caliber. He went back toward Cab Cabin in a hurry, and the next thing we knew, a telephone call came through to headquarters to tell us for God's sake lay off, that General MacArthur was in the plane and please let him come home.

When he came back the second time we kept our fingers off our triggers, but his pilot abided by the rules this time and gave us a wide berth.

The fact that we were never reprimanded by our commanding General for almost rubbing him out was characteristic of him.

That incident seemed a long time ago on May 4. The General was gone now, and that last submarine which had brought us nothing and had only taken some of us away was a blow from which we never recovered. Many of the officers and men were low in their minds about it. They felt that they could have made out so wonderfully with such a little more. If, for instance, we had only had a pompom to replace that one lost on Malinta Hill or two or three more beach-defense guns, it would have made all the difference in the world.

On May 4 we worked feverishly all night long and well into the morning hours to finish widening that channel, as it seemed inevitable that the *Quail* had only a few more hours left, since she was the only ship still in commission.

But the eyes on the hills no longer followed our efforts.

On shore the marines had stopped talking about how long they were going to stick it and talked only of how many Japs they could get before they were rubbed out. The soldiers and sailors on Corregidor talked only of hunger and food.

On the afternoon of May 5, I was walking around and talking to the outpost on Malinta Hill. The Japs were after the *Quail* hot and heavy. Every few minutes a messenger came panting up the hillside to say that headquarters had sent him to tell me that the *Quail* was reported sunk. And each time I told the messenger to tell headquarters that the news of her sinking was premature. I was watching her from the top of the hill. I moved around so much I guess the messengers had a hell of a time finding me. We were supposed to be asleep, but, as tired as they were, most of the officers and crew couldn't keep their eyes closed. It twisted our insides to see the *Quail* lying out there so helpless against repeated Jap dive-bombing attacks, even if she was cold dead, without oil, and useless to us.

Some of the other men begged to be allowed to go out to her and man her two remaining machine guns. Headquarters said no but that maybe if she survived throughout the day they would say yes tomorrow. That was all we could do about it.

It was a miracle that she did survive. She suffered plenty of near misses—the kind of near misses that had ripped the *Pigeon*'s sides wide open and sunk her. But the *Quail* seemed to have a charmed life. She seemed to rear back on her anchor chain and dodge bombs, ahead, astern, and on both sides of her. The sun went down and she was still there with colors flying.

The Tunnel in the Rock

There was no mine sweeping for us that night, and we were scheduled to remain ashore, but we begged for permission to go out to the *Quail* and take along enough men to man the remaining guns in the morning. The Commandant finally consented, but we were only to take the minimum number of men necessary to man them and raise her steam for the few miles left in her should we chance to catch a Jap landing barge trying to come through South Harbor.

We picked up twenty-four men, plus our three officers and a visiting officer from the *Tanager* who came along as an unscheduled guest, because he was a good pal of our chief exec and because he felt homeless since his ship had been sunk two days before.

The *Tanager* was sunk on May 4 by shellfire from the Cavite shore. Jap dive bombers had given her a pasting but hadn't been able to sink her. However, six- or eight-inch shells blasted into her and set her on fire. Almost immediately she was a mass of flame from bow to stern, and her ammunition started blowing up. She got her death wallops at three o'clock. At four the ammunition began to go off. For the next two hours she rolled and tossed like a woman in labor, until her agony ended at six, when she went down by the stern. At sunset her bow went under too.

3

Sandbags and Fox Holes

WHEN THE Rock started to go it went fast. About two o'clock in the morning, my officer of the deck shook me by the shoulder and tried to wake me. He was trying to tell me the Japs had fired off a big white rocket and he didn't know what it meant. His voice seemed to reach me from afar off, but before he was finished the Japs began to pour it on Corregidor, and noise, solid and heavy as a jet of water, roared at me and woke me up.

Malinta Hill was looped with what looked like enormous strings of firecrackers going off, and explosions took hold of the air and shook it. From the deck of the *Quail*, I could hear shells miss the hill, hit the water, and ricochet, their rotating bands making a high, singing whine. Shell bursts, blinding yellow with red cores, banged on the hill and flowered into fiery petals of flame.

This heavy barrage went on for half an hour, when two more rockets went up and burst in a shower of trailing green sparks. The firing stopped, and I heard a voice say, "This is the works. This time they're playing for keeps." The voice had a familiar ring, and I realized it was my own.

Sandbags and Fox Holes

It wasn't hard to figure out that Jap troops were advancing during the lull. They must have taken Monkey Point before this last rain of shells and, as nearly as I could tell, were now trying to circle the base of Malinta Hill. When heavy rifle fire broke out on all sides of Malinta, including the south side where we were anchored, my hunch wasn't a guess any more.

I called the crew to action stations and we stood by.

At four-thirty a coded-voice radio message came through for us to move the twenty-four men of the *Quail's* crew over to Fort Hughes on Caballo Island. We opened the boiler safety valves and let the steam out in a roaring hiss of white vapor, turned off the oil jets under the boilers, yanked the breech blocks off the guns, threw them along with our rifles into our two ship boats, and shoved off. One of our boats was gas-powered. The other was a Diesel whaleboat.

The trip over to Caballo lasted an interminable fifteen minutes. The guns high up on Hughes were slamming stuff at the Japs on Monkey Point, and Hughes also had a battery of seventy-fives down near the water. We could hear its shells going over our heads. We ducked as they passed and afterward there would be a blast on Monkey Point.

I tried to conjure up pictures in my mind of the destruction they worked when they landed. I imagined myself a Jap hearing them coming, wondering if one of them had my name written on it, and then as they went off, no more wondering—just nothingness. It made very satisfactory imagining. But I also wondered if, in the confusion, one of our own isolated groups of marines and soldiers was still holding out on Monkey Point, where those shells were landing. That wasn't as good a picture and I had to blank it out from my mind.

I figured we'd be lucky to make Caballo dock without somebody on Fort Hughes getting the idea we were a Jap landing party and letting us have it. Certainly they had a right to be hair-triggered with Bataan gone and parts of Corregidor nibbled away. My flashlight had a shield, so it would flash in one direction only, and I worked it for all I was worth, dot-dashing our recognition signal.

After we reached the dock and unloaded the crew, we hauled the gas boat back out into South Harbor and anchored her to keep our two boats separated so that they wouldn't both be sunk by the same shell or bomb. Then we parked the whaleboat under Caballo dock and walked along its concrete floor toward the first defense trench, yelling like crazy and waving our arms. We figured it didn't make much difference what we yelled as long as it sounded like English and not Japanese, so even as we yelled we tried to enunciate our words clearly. I can't remember any of those words. I forgot them immediately if I ever knew what they were. We just opened our throats and let them out. We felt helpless and vulnerable. Our legs seemed hollow and weak and not much use in the business of keeping us marching steadily forward. The seventy-fives and the mortar in the pit higher up on the island were kicking up such a racket, there was a better than even chance our men in the trench might not even hear our yelling.

But we made it. We found out later that the seventy-five battery was manned by the part of our own crew we had turned over to the Army Command weeks before, when

Sandbags and Fox Holes

we first started stripping the *Quail* down. They recognized us and tipped off the defense trench sentries to let us through.

Once past the trench we went up a winding trail to the entrance of headquarters tunnel. The tunnel ran through Caballo, sloping upward through the hill four hundred feet to Fort Hughes.

Head, my pharmacist's mate, and I were the last ones to enter, and just as we started in we heard bombs coming. They came at us making noises like a freight car coming around a bend up the line. They got louder and louder, until you could hear wheels rattling over invisible rail joints. The sixth sense you develop about bombs told us they were going to be close, so we dived into the tunnel mouth and landed sprawling on top of men in the last stages of exhaustion. They were too weary to move, even when we fell on them. They didn't curse or protest or try to shove us off. They merely grunted.

When the bombs stopped bursting outside, we started up the tunnel once more. The naked electric bulbs strung along the top were switched off, but there was a sickly before-sunrise radiance from the openings at the tunnel's ends. The floor was covered with blurred figures lying down or sitting with their backs to the tunnel walls. Their heads hung down and they stared at the floor. It was hard not to step on them or bump into them, but they were too tired to complain. As we went along, some of them summoned up enough energy to grab our arms and pull us this way and that so we wouldn't fall.

Each man in the tunnel had a dirty rag wrapped around his face and nose. The dust was ten times worse than it had been in the Corregidor tunnels, and we soon discovered that if we wanted to breathe at all we would have to get rags and wrap them around our faces, too.

The lateral passageways opening off the tunnel to the left let in a murky half-light from the mortar pits. It was terribly hot in the place, and there wasn't any talk going on. There was a low, muttered undertone made up of broken snatches of conversation, beginning nowhere and ending nowhere. I soon began to find out why. The heat and dust of the place choked you, and the noise coming in at each end of the tunnel and the shattering crack of the mortars going off chopped your words short and threw part of them away. Our own voices sounded to us like the voices of feeble old men who had been ill for a long time.

When a bomb landed topside, it reminded me how it had been in a subway back home when a surface train rolled overhead, and I had a fleeting moment of fear that the whole place was going to cave in on us.

After climbing awhile, we came to a place where men weren't packed together quite so solidly, and I told my crew to sit down while I went up and found the control room.

The men gathered in that room wore long slacks and khaki shirts open at the neck. The slacks and shirts were filthy, faded, and grease-stained. Their insignia of rank was virtually indistinguishable. It was hard to tell a private from a sergeant or a sergeant from a colonel. Their eyes were bloodshot from lack of sleep and from whirling, penetrating clouds of dust. Shaving had gone out—they wore beards of twelve assorted sizes, shapes, and colors—and their teeth showed white through grime and straggly whiskers.

From somewhere back inside of me a little rush of Army-Navy Game Day pride rose up, and I thought, "I mustn't let these babies think the Navy has its tail dragging."

I recognized Lieutenant Colonel Hopkins, drew myself up as smartly as I could, and said, "The crew of the U.S.S. *Quail* reporting for duty," just as they do it in the movies.

"How are your men?" Colonel Hopkins asked. "Are they in good shape?"

By comparison with the men we had seen as we came through the tunnel my men seemed very fit indeed. I said, "They're top of the morning, Colonel."

His mouth worked itself into a grin. "I'm glad to hear it because we've got a good job for you. Colonel Foster will tell you about it."

In the corner was a telephone switchboard, the kind you see in the lobby of any Park Avenue apartment house. Next to it stood a good-sized, flat-topped table with dirty maps and artillery diagrams tacked down so that the sudden lift of high-explosive concussion wouldn't blow them away. Along one side was a still larger switchboard, in front of which a man wearing headphones stood, shoving a plug in and out and talking to people in the control rooms still left on Drum and Corregidor and Fort Frank.

There were also a signal-light apparatus on which lights flashed from time to time from the batteries still in working order, and several long tables where Army decoding officers sat slumped down, working in fits and starts. As each minute went by, there was less for them to do.

In one wall was a jagged hole blown through four feet of solid concrete; it led into the mortar pit. Through the gap I could see one mortar still intact.

Colonel Hopkins was slight and small-boned. He had sand-colored red hair, a red beard, and the kind of scholarly face that looks as if it ought to be wearing glasses even when it isn't.

He pulled at Colonel Foster's sleeve, who tore off his earphones and cocked his head on one side to listen.

"This is Lieutenant Commander Morrill," Colonel Hopkins said.

Colonel Foster looked at me and asked, "Is that right?"

I nodded. I could see his beard wiggle and I knew another smile was trying to get through the hairy foliage.

"These Navy titles always get me mixed up," he explained.

Foster was heavy and solid, with thin lips on a broad face. He was worrying a burned-out cigar stub with his teeth and looked like the traditional tough Army colonel of the fiction writers and Hollywood casting directors.

"The Colonel wants your boys to man the final defense line," he said. "You'll find it down below, just outside the mouth of the tunnel." I remembered the bombs that had launched me into my swan dive on top of the exhausted men.

"Did you bring any guns with you?" he asked.

I told him my men had their rifles and pistols.

"Well, just man the trench outside of the tunnel and after everything else has been knocked out, you're supposed to keep the Jap landing force out of here."

I went back out into the tunnel, called my crew together

again, and told them about it. Just then two stretcher cases were brought along on their way to the hospital, and somebody asked, "Where'd they get it?"

The Army Medical Corps men carrying them said, "We picked them up down by the final defense line."

The men looked at me and I looked at them. We didn't say anything but just went back through the tunnel and sat down in the trench we had passed coming up from the dock. Even in the short time since we had seen it last, it looked different. It never had been much. Now it was just a shallow trough chewed out of all resemblance to a trench.

We hadn't been there long before Colonel Foster sent for us to come back up once more. When we finished the climb, he looked us over again. "So you boys are pretty strong, eh?" he asked. Pointing to the gap in the wall and showing us two wooden sidings about three feet apart, he said, "I've had my carpenters build up the sides of a sand barricade here. I want your crew to fill it up with loose sand. There's plenty of sand out there in the mortar pit spilled around from broken sandbags."

I got the gang together and we went out into the mortar pit, found two or three worn-out shovels, and started to pitch the sand in.

Sweat gummed our shorts to our thighs and stung our eyes. Our muscles began to ache and flutter like the nerves of teeth in need of fillings. I could see my crew fading rapidly. I sat down to try to figure out how we could do the job with less wear and tear. Then I got it. If we threw sandbags into the barricade without emptying them, it would save a lot of time and effort. The Colonel, I thought, is a nice guy, but nuts—he's got us doing this the hard way.

So we threw in about twenty-five bags. There was about a forty-foot run across the mortar pit to get a bag. Then we'd run back between bombs and dump it.

A stick of bombs hit the lip of the pit, and we scrambled down under the mortar. When the air stopped shivering we put our heads up once more, and a soldier said, "I believe you boys would be more comfortable if you hide out in the shell room here." He said it slowly but with a little hesitation between each word, like the King of England trying to conquer his stammer. We noticed a narrow opening around a concrete corner we hadn't seen before, partially covered by half a steel door. The rest of the door had been blown away.

The Jap shells came in, in bursts of two or three, and we tried to time it so we could make it to the shell room while they were going off. One of the gang would yell, "Scram!" We'd jump for shelter and sweat there listening to the shrapnel rattling on the steel door when one of the shells landed in the pit. Then, slowly, like turtles, we'd stick our heads out, survey the damage, shove the door open, and tear out after another bag. Sometimes we didn't quite make it and lay flat on the rubble, grabbing at loose concrete to hold us down. After a direct hit, the dust and debris hung in the air for a long time before it settled, and there was almost total darkness outside in the huge, square, well-like place before we could breathe once more.

We were still heaving sand when a sergeant said, "Get clear," and we ducked back toward the shell room, thinking more bombs were coming. A little dried-up mite of a man yelled in a voice startlingly big for such a little punk, "*Luzon* crew, man your mortar." Up from nowhere—apparently out of mashed-up concrete—came a single file of ghosts. Dog-trotting along, half staggering, dragging their feet after them, heads down, their eyes watching their feet. They went about the business of getting the mortar ready like zombies or sleepwalkers rather than appearing to think about what they were doing.

From an alcove we didn't even know was there, they trundled a little truck with a shell on it and dragged powder out the same way. Some of them took hold of the mortar-training and elevating mechanism and spun wheels around to depress it so they could load it. Three or four of them got behind the shell with a ramrod and rammed it home.

It went smoothly enough. There was no lost motion; the net result couldn't have been better if they had all been robust and bursting with health and vigor, instead of being the weirdest-looking bunch of scarecrows I ever hope to see. As a matter of fact, I never again in my lifetime want to see men so utterly used up as they were. It haunts you afterward.

We stopped filling a bag and watched them, open-mouthed. Knowing they were sailors and not coast artillerymen at all, we wondered how they'd learned to do the job so smoothly.

The shell went home with a little clank of metal on metal. They punched the powder bags in; back went the powder and shell cart to its place in the wall. There were shouted words sounding like, "Elevation two six nine... Azimuth zero one five"—and the man on the gun turned cranks. Then altogether, just as they had come in, they shuffled out of sight, still in Indian file.

In sixty seconds the world exploded around us. The

island seemed to rock. Light bulbs blew out of their sockets. Things tossed around like objects doing St. Vitus' dance during an earthquake. It was ten times worse than the worst explosion we had ever heard. I put my fingers up to my ears, expecting to find blood oozing from broken eardrums. The dust and smoke left us in a complete blackout. No dust storm in the Dust Bowl could have touched it. When at last we could see each other again, one of my crew looked at me dazed and asked, "What the hell was that?"

One of the others told him. "You fool, that was the mortar going off, they fire it by remote control."

About eight o'clock we slammed the half-portion door once more and waited for the usual dust cloud to clear away. When it was gone we saw our laboriously constructed sand barricade spread out in a low mound. I crawled up on the mound, put my head into the control room, and asked, "Colonel, are you all right?"

He didn't produce a grin this time, "You didn't take the sand out of the bags, did you?" he asked. And carefully, as though talking to a child, he explained that when there are gaps and small openings between bags, shrapnel gets into them and splits them wide open.

When he was through, he said, "Now go ahead and build it up again."

I asked him if my crew could have time out for breakfast. We had come away from the *Quail* in a hurry and we were beginning to feel empty.

"Go down into lateral tunnel eighteen," he said. "They'll fix you up, only have your men take it in relays. Half of you work here while the other half eats. We don't want the switchboard in here knocked out."

"What about you and Colonel Hopkins and the rest?" I asked.

"The hell with your blarney," he said. "I'm busy. Right now I can't get headquarters on Corregidor."

"What's the trouble?" I asked. "Are the cables broken?"

"I can get through all right," he said, "but all I can get is an orderly on the other end. I can't seem to find out where General Wainwright and his staff are."

We didn't know it then, of course, but if the Jap newspapers we saw later were right, General Wainwright and his staff had gone to inspect the fighting on Monkey Point and advance Jap patrols had captured them. If that was the way it occurred, it was easy one-hand for the Nips. The General and his staff weren't even armed.

Half of my men started nailing the sidings back in place while I went into the control room to look for my friend, Pete Welch, a Navy pal of long standing. I found him in a little passage behind the power-generator room off the control room. Pete's job was to act as co-ordinator between the Navy troops stationed at Fort Hughes and the Army Command. In addition, the Army had put him in charge of power-plant installation.

I came up behind him and said, "What the hell, Pete, haven't you got any work to do? How about some breakfast?"

He squinted at me and said drowsily, "We do a few things up here from time to time, Jack. The only trouble is those sons-of-bitches won't let us sleep." He pointed to a hole in the wall less than a foot above his bunk, and picked up a hunk of shrapnel from under the bunk. "They sent this up this morning."

Shrapnel travels horizontally and that piece had come through the gap we had been trying to repair.

Pete got ahold of a couple of Filipino mess boys and asked them, "What have we got good to eat?"

With all that hell rumbling and spitting against their ears, they still managed a grin. "Good chow right away," they said.

Lieutenant Commander Brooks, the skipper of the *Luzon*, showed up—there were some other officers I'd never seen before—and we sat down for breakfast. The good chow turned out to be the same old canned salmon and rice. Evidently, Pete's question, "What have we got good to eat?" was a standing joke among them.

Pete's filtered water, of which he was so proud, was an inch of sooty fluid in the bottom of the glass. He had patched machinery together using gumption and old parts, and somehow fashioned a distillation plant for the fort which changed sea water into fresh, drinkable stuff.

But in the last few weeks the Japs had managed to destroy almost all of his water tanks. He was griped about it, but not discouraged.

"If the Nips would let up on us for a couple of hours, I'd put that machinery so far underground they'd never be able to hit it," he said.

After breakfast we tackled those sandbags once more. By this time I didn't care if I ever saw one again. They had begun to take on malevolent personalities of their own, and made me think of drunks who are limp and heavy and hard to handle and keep flopping out of your hands if you relax your grip even for a second. Finally, we had the barricade about four-fifths full of loose sand and whatever else we could pitch into it, when another load of bombs came rumbling down and knocked it flat again. Once more I put my head through the hole into the control room and asked, "How are you?"

The Colonel's face was grimier, if possible, and his teeth showed even whiter. "Let me look at that thing," he said disgustedly.

He studied it for a while and asked, "Where are your reinforcing wires, Commander?"

I looked at him blankly.

"You're supposed to have three sets of wires reinforcing those planks to keep the thing from opening up like a pudding when the strain comes," he explained.

I said apologetically, "We didn't see any around."

His beard wiggled and the grin came back from its hiding place in his whiskers.

"Don't you gobs know *anything?*"

"I guess we've got webbed feet, Colonel," I told him. "I've never heard of reinforcing wire before."

He had his carpenter show us how to do it properly, and about ten-thirty we got the thing finished for the last time. My men were back in the tunnel, resting as best they could. Two of them were lying on the tunnel floor when a red-hot scrap of shell fragment landed between them and burned through their clothing. Each one of them thought the other had pinched him. They were mad enough to start trading punches, and the expression on their faces when they found out what had caused their anguish was ludicrous.

It seemed a good time for me to take a look-see and find out if the *Quail* was still afloat. So I climbed the last steep part of the tunnel to the topside end. After I got there, there was still a hundred-foot climb among loose rocks and gravel ahead of me until I reached a ledge gouged out of solid rocks in the side of the cliff. I had often wondered why they called Corregidor the Rock when Caballo looked so much more like Gibraltar. I remember a life-insurance ad featuring England's huge fortress sentry standing with its feet in the Mediterranean. Caballo looked enough like it to have posed for the ad.

The ledge was three quarters of the way to the top, and on it a spot big enough to hold a seventy-five-millimeter field gun had been cleared away. The fox hole behind it was meant as shelter for the men who served the piece. Packed into the hole now were three or four men—their legs, arms, and bodies fantastically scrambled. I felt naked and alone up there in spite of having them for company. Shells were splitting the air open and sending ragged hunks of rock rocketing up when they hit. I had made up my mind to run all the way up to the very top of the path, when a marine corporal hooked his fingers into my shirt collar and pulled me down into the fox hole, head-first. It happened so quickly I didn't know what the score was or what it was all about. And I stayed in that position with my head under shelter and my rump sticking out for a minute or two before I could back out and ask the corporal, "What's the idea of giving me the bum's rush?"

"I'm sorry, sir," he said stiffly. "I was afraid you might get hit."

"You don't look like Superman," I told him. "Why didn't you hole-up, too?"

"I'm used to it," he said. "When I hear one coming I'll

Sandbags and Fox Holes

be in that hole along with you if I have to use a shoehorn. You might have been a second too late." Our ears picked a warning screech out of the din, and he yelled, "Duck!"

This time I crawled into the hole without having to be yanked in. The marine scuttled in behind me on all fours. When my eyes got used to the place I could make out what the other box holders looked like. Immediately before me was a man wearing a chief petty officer's cap, and I asked him what ship he was from.

He told me, and added, "We're not doing so hot."

My marine chaperon wasn't so downhearted. "If we can clean up the Nips on Monkey Point, we'll be all right," he said.

But the chief petty officer wasn't so optimistic. "Yeah?" he said. "Maybe we can hold 'em off for another week, but then what? What's the use?"

He wasn't my man and I wasn't responsible for his morale, but his line of reasoning was something I was trying not to admit to myself, and if I stuck around and listened to that kind of talk I wouldn't be able to hold it off.

I walked to the edge of the ledge and took a good look at the *Quail*. Over by Corregidor there was so much smoke and splashing I couldn't see much. The Japs were shelling Corregidor's middle side and topside. They were shelling Caballo, too, under my feet and around me, but not with a complete barrage. Not yet.

I took another look around the harbor, saw the forty-foot gasoline boat from the *Quail* still afloat, and went back to the control room.

4

Escape from Caballo

TENSION lived in that control room like a physical presence. The men in command were trying to visualize the things happening to Corregidor and what those things meant to Fort Hughes. Their power plant was knocked out. Their water system was gone. Bomb loads were smashing into their mortar pits, and they were sending sergeants around to find out which of their guns were blown up and which were still usable. Each time when the word came back, it was more disheartening.

At ten forty-five an orderly reported to Colonel Foster that the lookout had sighted several white flags on Corregidor. Just then a coded message came through from the Rock ordering the Colonel to destroy the contents of all safes. The Colonel double-checked on the message, but although it had come from Corregidor the Colonel couldn't find out who on the Rock had sent it.

Five minutes later white flags were reported on Fort Drum and Fort Frank. Colonel Foster turned to his fire-control sergeant and said, "We haven't any white flags, have we, Jones?"

"No, sir," Jones told him, "we haven't. We've never made any up."

"We're not going to make any up unless we get orders to," the Colonel told him.

I began to wonder what we were going to do about the *Quail* waiting out there in South Bay for the Japs to come and get her, and at eleven o'clock radio-telephone orders came through that the Navy Commandant on Corregidor had ordered all ships scuttled.

Thinking that perhaps there was a chance the Commandant was in Jap hands and they were dictating the order, I looked up Brooks, the skipper of the *Luzon* I had had breakfast with along with Pete Welch, and together we asked for verification. We couldn't get it. There was a dead silence at the Corregidor end of the radio. We stood there for a while, discussing whether or not we should consider the order authentic.

It had been previously arranged by the Commandant that if worst came to worst and it was necessary to issue a scuttle-ship order, he would have a profusion of multi-colored rockets and other pyrotechnic materials set off from the escape tunnel on Malinta Hill. We asked Colonel Foster if his lookout station had noticed such a display. The lookout reported that a short time before he had seen what looked like a super-dooper Fourth-of-July outburst blossoming on Malinta. Brooks and I looked at each other and said, "Well, I guess that's it."

"The *Luzon* and the *Oahu* are total wrecks now," Brooks said. "They'll probably sink very shortly anyhow. Suppose I send one man out from each ship with you? They know the right valves to open if they can get at 'em. After you scuttle the *Quail*, how about putting my men aboard the *Luzon* and *Oahu* to see if they can sink them any faster than they're already sinking?"

I went out into the tunnel, found my executive officer, asked him to get a scuttling party together, picked out eight men to go with me, and we went down the tunnel.

The men huddled against the rough concrete walls didn't even look up when we barged past them this time. When we asked one of them a question, he looked at us with a dull, unseeing look. When they heard a bomb screeching down outside, they roused themselves temporarily, rolled over, covered their heads with their arms, and put their faces against the concrete floor until it was over. They had been under very heavy shelling for a week and subjected to a kind of Jap adaptation of the Chinese water torture, only done with high explosives jiggling the spinal fluid and scrambling the gray matter inside of the brain pan instead of slowly falling drops of water. Then, too, they had been under pretty heavy shelling for three weeks before that. There were no relief replacements to take their places. And they hadn't had any sleep.

They had had to man their guns day and night, and any city copper who specializes in third-degreeing can tell you what no sleep does toward breaking even the strongest man and rendering him helpless. If by some miracle they did manage to snatch an hour or two, it was merely their cue to crawl wearily to their feet and man their guns again.

Pausing in the lower tunnel entrance, we could see shells the size of seventy-fives falling between us and the dock.

I split the men up into two parts, and we made our dash —following the narrow path down, running hard, breath sobbing in our throats. There were concrete steps with wide treads, then the path went through a dirt cut and bent around toward the dock along a broad graveled pathway.

Shells were falling farther up the hill and over beyond on the A.A. batteries, and light machine-gun fire was crackling through the island area. The water was full of spouts jumping where shells were falling. But the Japs laid off the path long enough for us to make our sprint. One of our men, Spencer, was puffing and blowing. He was a World War veteran who had put on a lot of weight since he had been a seventeen-year-old infantryman, slim enough to fit into an Argonne trench. When we got to the dock, we found a big hole in the dock where we had left the whaleboat. Looking down through the hole, we saw our boat, in two pieces, resting on the bottom in twenty feet of water. It lay there seeming to tremble a little in the green-blue depths, and a punch-drunk fish whipped crazily between it and our eyes.

The men asked, "Well, Captain, what'll we do now?" It was a question they had asked a thousand times in the past and would ask a thousand times more before we were through.

I didn't know. But one of them came through with an answer. "Why can't we get the Army to open up with any guns they've got left and sink our ships for us? We wouldn't last five minutes out there in a boat, even if we had a boat."

"O.K.," I said. "We'll go back to the tunnel and see if we can sell 'em the idea."

So we went back, uphill this time. Spencer's face was the color of an eggplant. His tongue dangled to his chin.

When he could talk he said, "One run like this is enough for me. I can't make another." We left him behind next time, almost out on his feet. His spirit was willing, but his flesh was a ball and chain dragging at his legs.

Once more I went up to Colonel Foster's headquarters and asked him, "How about the Army helping us do our sinking? Our whaleboat's sunk. We left it under your dock and the Nips put a shell through the dock and the boat, too. Our ships are lying broadside to you now. If you can hit 'em amidship just about the water line I don't think it would take more than three or four shots to give 'em the business."

"I've only got one battery left," he said. "I'll check to see if it can bear in your direction, but I don't think it can."

"How about that battery shooting at us on the way over this morning?" I wanted to know.

"We lost them this morning, right after you landed," he said.

It brought me up short with a tourniquet of constricted muscles around my throat. The men we had loaned the Army had manned that battery.*

He checked his diagrams to see if C Battery could do us any good. "No soap," he said. "It'll only bear to seaward."

I didn't give up. "How about it if I take my gang up there and turn it around for you?" I suggested.

He was fast losing patience, and I didn't blame him. He had plenty on his mind, and, after all, scuttling the ships was our job, not his. "That would be about two weeks'

---

* For the information of dependents, these men were Filipino reserves picked up in Manila before the war and not part of the regular *Quail* crew brought out from Hawaii.

Escape from Caballo

work," he said. "You'll have to move a couple of boulders the size of a house to start with."

I gave up and left. If I had known I wouldn't see them again I would have put in more time saying good-by. They were a couple of swell Army officers.

I went into the power-plant room and talked it over with Brooks. I told him that the only boat anywhere around was the one we had anchored out about two hundred yards from shore and we'd have to swim.

"You'll never get away with it the way the dive bombers are strafing," Brooks said.

I thought about how lousy it would be if the *Quail* were captured and used against us, or put to work sweeping mines for the Japs.

"We'll get out there somehow if we have to walk along the bottom neck-deep in coral heads," I told him.

He wished me luck.

Out in the tunnel I found Taylor, the *Quail*'s gunnery officer, one of whose legs and feet had been almost eaten away by a tropical skin disease. He hobbled rather than walked. "Guns," I said. "The Army hasn't got any stuff that'll bear on the ship. We've got to go out there and scuttle her ourselves."

He was no conversationalist. He just said, "Uh-huh."

I started trying to find out which of our men could swim and located four—Cucinello, Meeker, Weinmann, and Steele—who said they could make it. We ran back through the barrage area, between the tunnel and the dock, and threw off all our clothes except for our shorts. Then I remembered something and asked Taylor, "Didn't the doctor tell you salt water on that leg would be curtains?"

He grunted again.

"You wait here," I told him. "The rest of us will go out and get the boat and bring it back here for you."

When I got the men in the water I found that they had stretched a point and none of them could swim more than ten feet.

Taylor couldn't stand it. "The hell with it. I'm going along," he said, and jumped in with us.

I saw a water-logged life jacket floating by, thirty feet away. I swam out to it, brought it back to the dock, and put it on Steele. There was a momentary lull in the shell-fire churning South Bay. In it Taylor and I started for the boat with Steele floundering behind us in the life jacket like a dying whale. We could feel the water quiver and shake when a bomb missed the forts and landed in it. It was a queer, empty, gone feeling, as though the earth were jiggling around on Atlas' shoulders. It made your stomach turn over, and I knew how that punch-drunk fish felt.

After Taylor's first strangling gasp when the water bit into him, he seemed to be making out all right.

We were as puny and hopeless an expedition as ever took off from any shore anywhere. There we were—one man who couldn't swim, another to whom the undertaking was excruciating agony, and myself—headed out through a patch of water in which dive bombers were stitching fancy patterns with bullets that ripped into the waves with sounds like tearing paper.

I was sure we'd never make it. I'd been in spots before in which I had been too close to death to feel good about it, but this time, I thought, was definitely the pay-off. In that moment I knew what fear was, all right. It was something that made the inside of your mouth dry up and tied your stomach into granny knots, and you lived only from second to second, each second lasting ten years. Then I got mad at the *Quail*, and that helped.

That blamed old tub is draped around our necks like an albatross, I thought. *It's dragged us into tight squeeze after tight squeeze without ever having asked us if we wanted to be dragged into them, and now at the end it's pulling us down to a choking death.*

We tried to take care of those dive bombers that were strafing us by pulling the old trick of ducking our heads under water to sell the Nips the idea we were hit. Some of the bullets came close to us, but, after all, each plane could only bear on us for a few seconds at a time, and all of their shots went wild.

Twenty feet away from the gasoline boat, it occurred to us we had another problem to solve. How in the name of all that was holy were we going to pull ourselves up over the edge of the boat when we got there? None of us had enough strength to clamber up over her side. I trod water and thought desperately. I guess one's mind plays funny tricks, because what popped into mine was a day near Honolulu when I had been out hiking with my two children, John and Jill, on Tantalus Mountain. It was a wonderfully clear day, with the birds singing and the air just fresh enough. We had come upon a peak made of volcanic stone, sheer and forbidding, but I wanted to climb it and take a look around to spy out the land for other possible hikes in the future.

I told the kids to wait for me. "It won't take very long," I promised. "I'll be right back down." But Jill wanted to go with me, even after I explained that she couldn't possibly make it. She was five years old and small for her age, thin, wiry, and bright-eyed.

So I started. Behind me as I climbed I heard her calling, "Wait for me, Daddy."

I yelled back over my shoulder for her to stay where she was, telling her once more, "You can't make it."

It was more of a climb than I had thought, and once or twice I wondered if I were going to pull it off myself. But after a while, with sweat dripping down into my eyes and utterly exhausted, I got to the top and flopped down, gasping.

As I lay there I heard the sound of sobbing coming closer and closer and turned to look back. There she was, just coming over the top of the steepest ledge, scrambling like an agile little monkey and crying her heart out. Once on top she rushed over and threw her arms around me, saying over and over, "I thought I'd lost you." I held onto her tightly and thought, "If a little five-year-old kid can get up here, *anything* is possible."

The whole scene went through my mind in the time it takes to tell one one-hundredth part of it, and when it was gone a bright light switched on in my mind. I remembered that this particular boat had been rebuilt as a landing-force boat, and that after reconstruction her rudder stuck out from her stern about a foot below the surface, to protect it from bullets. We stepped up onto that rudder and from there into the boat. The sun was beating down on its planking, and it felt red-hot to our tender feet. We hopped around, feeling blisters start to puff up, while Steele got the engine started.

The anchor was a seventy-five-pounder attached to a boat-chain anchor cable. Ordinarily, two men could have heaved it up with no difficulty, but the utmost efforts of all three of us put together hardly equaled the lifting power of one ordinary man in good shape. We tugged and strained until our eyes bulged and our muscles cracked, but that hook felt as if it were lodged under the very backbone of Corregidor. Little by little, with sweat streaming from us, stinging our eyes and making our hands slippery, we eased the chain up until it cleared the bottom. Then we secured it and left it dangling while we went back to the dock to pick up the others.

The Japs were in the groove now, and shells were slamming against the sides of Caballo Island. Machine guns gave out their fast, sharp stuttering, and the air was full of big silver vultures painted with the rising sun, peeling off to lay their eggs on us. When a stick of bombs hit the water, the concussion jarred the base of our brains and made us feel as if our heads were coming open. In the middle of all that crackling hell the men we'd left behind tumbled aboard and helped us bring the anchor up the rest of the way. I didn't have to tell them to huddle out of sight behind the gunwales. They did it instinctively, although shell splinters or machine-gun slugs would have cut through the boat like a hot poker going through lard if they had come our way. The urge is born in you to be behind something, no matter how futile the protection it offers, when the enemy is slinging stuff your way.

We eased around that long dock, keeping it between ourselves and Corregidor as long as we could. Then, sucking in a deep breath and holding it, we gave her a full throttle and made a dash westward. The half-sunken hulls of the *Luzon* and the *Oahu* were spaced in such a way that we could use them as relay stations in working our way over to the *Quail*. The way we doped it, if we could get in behind the *Oahu* we'd be screened for the moment from the Jap gunners on Corregidor. Then, if we were still in the land of the living, we could try for the *Luzon* and, after another pause, make our last sprint for the *Quail* itself.

But we reckoned without our pals, the dive bombers, cavorting in the air over us. A couple of them caught sight of us and thought we looked like easy pickings. As they zoomed over us with the air shrilling against their fuselage, I told the men to take to the floor boards as if they had been hit. Taylor and I set the rudder at ninety degrees, which sent the boat swinging in a circle and made her look as if she were out of control, but at the same time we managed to give the tiller an occasional nudge that would bring her up behind the *Oahu*, where we wanted to be. The dive bombers, apparently thinking we were knocked out, went off for other fish to fry.

After lying low for a few minutes, we nosed out from behind the *Oahu* and, feeding the engine all the gas it could eat, we made our bid for the *Luzon*. Coming out from behind the *Luzon*, the Japs let us have it, and we ran into a rain of machine-gun bullets. Somehow we lived through it, I suppose because we were at the extreme range of the Jap machine guns.

Once behind the *Quail*, the fire was blanked off, and we made fast alongside and climbed over her rail. Weinmann and Steele went down into the engine room and broke open two of the sea-chest castings with a sledge hammer. Meeker

Escape from Caballo

clambered down the fireroom ladder to open the eight-inch flood valves. Taylor and Cucinello began to cut fuses for a demolition charge in the magazine. While this was going on, I paid a flying visit to the charthouse. What the boys were doing down below got results, and quickly. The ship gave a convulsive lurch and seemed about to roll over. *A fine thing*, I thought, *if we've got through all of this only to have the old lady suck us down with her and hold us there while she kicks the bucket. A fine thing.*

I went back down that ladder and yelled for Taylor to get out of the magazine. Slowly, after what seemed centuries, his head reappeared.

"I just wanted to do a good job of it," he explained mildly.

The others were already over the rail and going down the rope ladder.

The *Quail* was still enough afloat to protect us from the guns on Corregidor, and we gathered our wits a little before we started back.

Far out near the seaward end of the Rock, enormous waterspouts reared up in long straight rows, half a mile long, each spout from two to three hundred feet high. Our Army on Corregidor was blowing up its land-controlled mines by pushing buttons in the control-room stations on the topside of Corregidor.

Near at hand it must have been terrific. If we had been out there near it, it would have caved in our lungs by the sheer power of its concussion. The mines weighed about half a ton each, and there were about 150 of them in each line. Normally, we would have heard a muffled thunder and felt the shock, but with so many other explosions all over the area, the effect was like seeing a silent movie of Niagara falling uphill.

The time was just about right for the question, "What'll we do now, Captain?" to come up, and up it came. Somebody always managed to spring it when it was hardest to answer, and I would be forced to meet it.

"We're going to pick up the rest of the *Quail* gang, hide out here until after dark, and get away from this place," I told them.

I took a look over to our right and saw that our Diesel boat was still anchored in the middle of South Harbor, where we'd left her after our last stint of mine sweeping. I think that even when we left her there I must have had it in the back of my mind that in the end she might be a thirty-six-foot gangplank to freedom for us. Now I found myself counting on it.

Steele was standing beside me, keeping the engine idling. "Looks to me like Caballo'd be kind of a hard place to go back to right now," he drawled, and pointed up at a white flag hanging limply over it. We stood there looking at it unbelievingly.

Somebody said, in a dull tone as if talking to himself, "It wasn't there when we left Caballo dock."

"How about it if we get in behind the *Ranger* and lay low and see what happens?" Meeker asked. Battered and deserted, the tug *Ranger* had been beached on Caballo and her crew sent ashore some weeks before.

I told Meeker it was a great idea. If we could do it, it would be the neatest trick of the week for us, or of any other week of our entire lives.

"We'll pretend we're going back to Caballo dock," I

said, "and if we get a clear spell we'll slide in behind her."

For the first part of our run we were shielded from the Jap batteries on Corregidor by the *Quail*. After that we could hear shells going over our heads and making us duck with their "chug-chuggy-chug-chug" sound, the chugging faint at each end and louder in the middle. One dive bomber made a pass at us, but he evidently thought we'd be Jap meat when they landed on Fort Hughes and he didn't put his back in it. It didn't hit us, but it did connect with a poor old Filipino 680 boat, a tiny steam tug almost as small as our launch. When the slugs ripped through her, a frightened brown face popped up and looked around to see what was going on. Then the face went down and out of sight. A hundred yards away from the dock and about the same distance from the *Ranger*, we got a comparatively quiet interval and edged in behind the tug.

Bent double, we moored our boat to her in such a way that it would look tip-tilted and half stove in, and, scrambling across the tug's deck, we piled into her after deckhouse. Soon we were going over her to see if we could find anything useful to help us in escaping.

The first thing we bumped into was four automatic rifles and six Springfields, and we made our plans to use them if the Japs came out in a small boat to board us. We wouldn't fire at them as they approached, nor would we even cut them down as they came overside. If we did that, we ran the risk that some of them might make a getaway and go back for help. From the afterdeck two long dark passageways led into the ship's interior. We'd be there, waiting for them at the far end of each of those passageways. At that distance we couldn't miss.

The *Ranger*'s upper cabin had bamboo screens over the windows. We cut small holes in these screens and stationed two men there, one on each side of the ship. The first place I visited, searching for helpful articles, was the chartroom. By dint of much sorting, I managed to get together several charts covering all the possible routes we might use in getting through the Philippines. But search as I would, I could find no chart of the Dutch East Indies or Australia, except one large-area, small-scale chart of the Western Pacific.

We took a sextant and two pairs of binoculars. I dug up dividers, parallel rules, pencils, and pads of paper to help with navigation. I found a copy of the *Nautical Almanac*, but I could find no Bowditch and no hydrographic publications, either for celestial navigation or for coastal piloting. We were fairly familiar with the Philippines, but I knew if we ever had to go to the Dutch East Indies we wouldn't be very much better off than Columbus was when trying to discover America, so far as knowing anything about winds, currents, and, above all, the weather was concerned.

The lookouts sent out alarms from time to time. Steele summoned us once, and we came running. He was peering through his slot in the bamboo screen, muttering to himself. A boat had left Corregidor, packed with Filipino civilians, and carrying large white flags in the stern and bow. But after heading in our direction, it turned eastward. Two or three small motor launches followed it, similarly loaded.

Still another boat left the dock at Corregidor and went in the direction of Fort Drum. It also carried white flags, and its passengers were white instead of brown. It disappeared around the corner of Caballo Island and twenty or twenty-five minutes later came back to Corregidor, so we figured its crew must have been acting as emissaries for the Japs and bearing surrender terms.

I don't think I'll ever again hear that line from the *St. Louis Blues*, "I hate to see that evenin' sun go down," without remembering how fervently we pulled for the sun to go down that afternoon. I noticed that my jaw muscles were aching and didn't know why. I discovered I had clamped my teeth together so hard, concentrating on helping pull that big red-hot ball down by sheer mental concentration, that the lower part of my face was suffering from cramps. The most important thing in life, it seemed to us, was that slowly lessening triangle formed by our eyes, the sun, and the point the sun was dropping toward. I think we all prayed a little to help it along. We were in a neck-or-nothing race, and whether we would lose it or not depended on whether it would go down before the Japs came in force to Fort Hughes.

All through the afternoon, occasional bursts of rifle and machine-gun fire came from Corregidor's bottomside and climbed higher up the Rock.

About four or four-fifteen, just when it seemed that the sun might actually go down that year instead of ten years in the future, the last of the boats roaming around South Harbor appeared. Sunset was due about six-thirty, and we had only two hours to go.

Steele gave up his loud, sibilant "His-s-s-t!" "This one," he reported, "is really coming toward us, and no fooling!"

We took our action stations and cuddled the automatics in our arms. For a while it seemed that Steele had called it right and that within eight minutes a boatload of Japs would be walking down a couple of dark passageways toward death. But 150 yards away from us, the boat swerved and went over to Caballo dock. It was a covered boat and there were sunken ships in our line of view, but as nearly as we could tell, two Japs got out of it, leaving two more in the boat. The ones that had disembarked went on up the dock, and one of our men, holding aloft a white flag, came down the hill to meet them. In twenty minutes all four Japs went back to Corregidor again.

The Filipino 680 the dive bomber had ripped open had had its bow knocked off, and the old Filipino we had thought wounded or dead poured himself out of her wreckage into a cockleshell of a boat four feet long and rowed over to the dock at Caballo.

The *Ranger*'s skipper had hidden a little four-oared rowboat away in a small cave the water had scooped out under the overhanging rocks on Caballo. Now, while we watched, four of the *Ranger*'s men got into it and rowed along past us, hugging the shore, and went over to the Caballo dock, too, and on up the hill. We never did find out why they had been hidden under the rock, whether they had seen us board the *Ranger*, or why they didn't join us instead of heading for Fort Hughes.

All afternoon Jap dive bombers had been having fun over Corregidor and Caballo. Later on that night, when we picked up our men from Caballo, we found that these playful Nips had killed a number of soldiers and sailors congregated at the ends of the tunnel on Fort Hughes, and the Jap heavies had laid out a lot more of them.

Then, about five o'clock, they really let go on Caballo and smothered her, attacking with waves of heavy planes in formations of nine. We were only fifty yards away from the island. It was a clear, sunny day. Yet we couldn't see the beach at all when the heat was turned on. Smoke rolled up as from all the oil tanks in the world on fire, and an inferno of sound dwelt in the somber cloud. The first two waves of planes had the range on the mortar pits down to a fine point, but the third was careless and managed to miss the island completely. When we heard those freight cars coming once more, we hit the deck. They landed so close to us that the flash of their detonation licked across inside the tug from window to window. Lying there, we felt as if we were lifted ten feet above the deck plates before falling back again. For a half-hour afterward we had ringing noises in our ears and felt dizzy from shock.

Finally, when the fire and smoke and noise enveloping Caballo died away, we peered out and saw that the *Luzon* and the *Oahu* had been hit again, and the Japs had almost finished the scuttling we had wanted to do for Brooks.

Between alarms, the men had done a good job of ransacking the tug, covering it with a fine-tooth comb from one end to the other. They had dug up four drums of Diesel oil, a fleece-lined Mackinaw, a number of blankets, several cases of corned beef, and canned salmon. There were a few choice cans of delicacies and one large can of tomato juice. When they had abandoned ship, the *Ranger* crew had left the remnants of their last meal right on the table. In one of the staterooms, we found a case of cigarettes. Last of all, we picked up a can of lubricating oil. When we were through we had a collection of junk piled on deck a pack rat or a jackdaw would have been proud of. We wrapped part of it up in a big khaki blanket to be shifted when darkness came, and put the sextants and the binoculars in another pile. When we had just about given up looking, we found a pile of dynamite with caps and fuses, and I put Taylor to work making grenades of them.

In spite of the convulsive pitch the *Quail* had given while we were trying to scuttle her, we watched her rolling and plunging in her death agony for two more hours before she gave up and went down by the stern with her bow sticking up. We worried about that air pocket holding up her bow, fearful the Japs could get a grip on her and raise her. But later on, Meeker, who was on watch, called out to me that even the bow was going. Tears ran down over his red face and his chunky chin and the blond, curly stubble on his cheeks. "I've been on that old lady for five years," he said. At the last, he looked the other way and refused to watch her final throes.

The sun was almost touching the water now. We pulled it down through those last ten degrees as if each of us had a rope tied to it and was busting a gut tugging. But even after sunset there remained an age-long twilight during which it was still too light to do anything about getting under way.

We sat around killing time by eating the food left on the *Ranger*'s table that hadn't spoiled. Taylor found a shower that ran fresh water and took a bath, washing the salt water from his sore leg and foot. When he was through, he put his dirty clothes back on and said, "Well, I hope that bath is going to last me longer than I think it's going to."

One more detail had to be settled. Who was to go back up into the fort at Caballo and get the rest of our men? I explained to the gang that I very definitely didn't want to go up there myself. Suppose, I explained, they give me orders to surrender and to surrender all of you people? So far we had been lucky. We had been away from the fort and out of communication with our own headquarters when the fatal moment had arrived. Being on my own I was entitled to make my own decisions. But suppose I went back up there and received a direct order to surrender from a superior officer? It wouldn't make any difference if the order came from an Army officer, I would still be bound by it. I could vaguely remember reading in some military lawbook that after a commander surrenders, his orders are no longer binding. However, there was no lawbook at hand nor any time to weigh a knotty legal technicality, and I preferred not to get involved in it.

The men agreed on my not going back up there. But when it came to one of them volunteering to do it, there were no volunteers. They would risk death willingly but not capture. However, they knew it had to be done, so they drew matchsticks for it. Cucinello drew the short matchstick. He loathed the idea and feared the job more than any of the really dangerous things he had done without a qualm. I instructed him to tell each *Quail* officer and man quietly that his captain wanted him, just that—nothing more and nothing less.

We got into our boat. There was a fairly heavy sea running, and we had a hard time throwing our gear in and getting in ourselves. Our next move was to go out to South Harbor to the Diesel boat, which we had made sure was still there during the last streaks of lemon-colored twilight. When we tried to start the Diesel's engine, it wouldn't do anything but lie down and play dead. I told Taylor and Weinmann to go back to the Caballo dock with Cucinello while he got the rest of the *Quail*'s men. "And be sure you get Richardson," I told Cucinello. "If anybody can get this engine perked up, it's him." Richardson wasn't chief engineer, and some of the other *Quail* engineers ranked him, but he had a gift for engines just as some people have a green thumb and can make plants grow in barren soil where no one else can.

Steele and I stayed behind and struggled with that cold block of pistons and valves, jamming our thumbs, splitting fingernails, and cursing softly under our breaths.

After a while, Steele somehow got the Diesel started and we went forward to try to get the anchor up. The cable ran out ninety fathoms deep, and we couldn't budge it even an inch, so we nursed the engine along and waited. About an hour later, we spotted our boat coming back once more. Cucinello had gone up into the tunnel and rounded up about twenty of the men we'd left there. He couldn't find one of our officers who had been sent off on a special job by the Army, but the *Tanager* officer who'd been visiting us came along.

Inside of the tunnel, Cucinello told me he had found our men lined up in ragged formation in the process of being disarmed by their officers. Rifles and pistols were being taken away from them. But some of our boys had managed to toss their pistols into the darkness behind them when the order came and had picked them up later. Some of them had seen us going out to the *Ranger* and had been hoping against hope we would come back for them. They had tried to hook some of the Army food for us instead of leaving it for the Japs, but they had been caught and the food taken away from them.

Escape from Caballo

Our bos'n's mate was disgusted because they had taken away his bos'n's knife. He regarded it as a kind of unofficial symbol of office and never ceased mourning its loss during the thirty-one days we were together afterward. During the afternoon, Cucinello said they had made our boys clean up the tunnel. In all likelihood it was a scheme thought up to keep the men's minds occupied, but somehow they got the idea they were cleaning it up for the Japs as part of the surrender terms and they were boiling mad about it.

After the gas boat tied up alongside of us, the *Tanager* officer came aboard and asked, "Captain, what are you up to?"

I told him I hadn't expected to see him, but if he wanted to go along with us and try to make a break it was O.K. with me. We'd be glad to have him.

"Where're you going?" he wanted to know.

I told him we were going to Mindanao, maybe Australia.

He was pessimistic about it. "You won't get thirty miles," he said. "Those destroyers out there are thicker than flies. They've been patrolling all day and all night for three weeks."

I just couldn't feel that way. I had had this moment in the back of my head for a long time, and a little gloomy talk didn't change my mind.

"I don't like the looks of the way the Japs are acting around here," he said. "But I *know* you boys are going to get killed."

I didn't want to argue, so I called out to the gang, "Let me have your attention just a second." And I gave them a speech. "You all know what the situation is. If you surrender without irritating the Japs too much they may treat you all right. On a logical basis your chances of remaining alive are probably better staying here, and some of our officers feel that escape is impossible. On the other hand, quite a few of you want to make the attempt, and if you want to try, I'm not going to ask you to stay here and surrender. I don't know exactly how we're going to do it but I've got an idea and I think I can get you through. You've got to hurry up and make your choice because we've got to get out of here damned fast if we're going."

Eleven of them piped up without any waiting and said, "We're all with you, Captain. Let's go."

The rest hung back, among them men for whom I have a great deal of respect. One of them was a petty officer. He summed it up for the ones who decided to stay. "I want to go," he said, "but I just haven't got the heart to make any more effort. I placed all my faith in the Rock not surrendering, and now that it has, it just seems that the bottom has fallen out of everything." His voice was dead, the voice of a man utterly without hope. It made me want to weep to hear it. It was heartbreaking.

"Maybe you'll get over it in a few hours," I suggested.

"No, Captain," he said, "I'd just be a drag on the party." He held out his watch. "Take this," he said and handed it to me. "It's a good watch and maybe it'll help you."

I didn't want his watch but I took it. I figured it would make him feel better if I did and let him think he had a stake in the project even if he couldn't bring himself to go along.

All of us, even those who weren't going, helped load the extra Diesel oil in the boat, which was a tough job with the boat bouncing and tossing and the men as weak as they were. The oil was in fifty-gallon drums weighing three hundred and fifty pounds each.

I had the men who were going get into the boat to test her loading capacity and found we had about six inches remaining above water, which was dangerous, but there wasn't much I could do about it. The boat had a compartment division about two thirds of the way aft, so that any water we shipped wouldn't roll up and down the boat but would be confined to the section in which it came over. It was powered by a Buda four-cylinder engine. Under the taffrail where the Diesel tanks were, we were to find storage space for other things such as coffee, sardines, and bananas. Usually, in peacetime, there were thwarts forward of the compartment division for liberty parties to sit on. But these thwarts were loose and could be taken out to make room for extra drums of Diesel oil and more stores.

In general, the boat was the kind that comes chugging up to Ninety-sixth Street in New York, with liberty parties on board when the fleet's in.

But I made a mental note to straighten out the tiller at the first possible opportunity, so the steersman could steer sitting down instead of standing up.

Then I thought of Head, our pharmacist's mate, and asked Cucinello if he had wanted to come. Cucinello said he hadn't been able to find him in the tunnel, but one of the men said, "I know the 'Doc' was counting on coming. He's been packed up and ready to go all afternoon." So I announced we were going back for him. Both boats got under way, the extra men helping to get the hook up. Corregidor was still under constant bombardment and there was a staccato roar of shells pounding home on Caballo.

When we reached the shattered dock for the last time, one of the men who had decided not to cast in his lot with us volunteered to go up and bring Head back. I also sent Rankin, just to make sure. Presently Rankin and Head came running down that dock faster than I'd ever seen either of them move before or since. Rankin jumped into the boat, and Head flung himself in on top of us. His chest heaved and his breath whistled in and out. "I thought you'd gone away and left me," he panted.

When Head could talk he gave me another picture of conditions back in the Fort Hughes tunnel. Being a pharmacist's mate he had naturally gravitated to the fort's hospital, or "sick bay" as he called it. During the afternoon when the men had grown careless, thinking their ordeal was nearly over, they had let down on their caution. As a result, during the all-out concentration of fire power around five o'clock, the casualties were so heavy the hospital was filled to overflowing and there was no time to keep things even halfway clean and orderly. The floor was slippery with blood, and the two doctors in charge operated continuously and frantically. There was too little time for the proper giving of anesthetics, but, according to Head, most of the wounded were so shocked they were insensible to pain. In addition to the two doctors, one Army Medical Corps man assisted them in that reeking, dust-ridden room. At one point during the afternoon, shrapnel had injured one of the two doctors and stunned the other. Then for three hours Head and the Army Medical Corps man took care of all of the cases alone, guided only by advice from the wounded doctor—who, with a three-inch gash in his skull, sat on the floor, propped against a wall—in the intervals when he was conscious. Head and the Corps man performed operations under pressure a skilled doctor would have been skittish about. But in the back of his mind all the time he was working, he told me, was the hope I wouldn't forget to come for him.

The worst part of it, Head said, had been the doctor who was stunned. "He just stood there by the operating table, clicking his teeth together hour after hour, not knowing what was going on or what the score was. I was scared stiff he'd grab a scalpel and get a cockeyed notion he ought to cut into some poor guy—clicking teeth and all."

The men on the dock said good-by and wished us luck with a mixture of feelings. A part of each one of them wanted to go, but the other part, the part now predominant, was already slipping down into the drugged relaxation of giving up, and a lessening of the tension they had lived under for weeks and months.

Many times afterward, we wished we had grabbed them and thrown them in with us whether they liked it or not.

Just as we were leaving, a Jap shell hit the far end of the dock, where the Army had a power plant and crane. That whole section caught fire and burned fiercely, with flames ribboning up into the sky.

Looking back, as we headed out to sea, at the figures of the ones we'd left behind silhouetted against the glow was one of the eeriest sights I've ever seen. Maybe it was the sudden gush of feeling at knowing that we were leaving a place in which I had more than half expected to die. Maybe the strain of the past days, with the super-strain of the last twenty-four hours piled on top, made me fey and lightheaded. Anyhow, I felt I was in a kind of never-never land somewhere between being alive and slipping over the edge of things.

5

Out to Sea

THE FLOOD of emotions churning in my mind when we shoved off from the dock calmed down, and I faced the purely practical problem of where to steer the boat. If we headed out through the channel we had cut in our own mine field it meant passing so close to the topside of Corregidor that the Japs would see us. And while we might get through the curtain of fire they'd throw around us, they'd stir up their picket boats farther out and put them on our tail. My hunch was that the danger of ending our getaway on a mine was a lesser one than that of bringing the Japs cracking down on us, so I headed southwest and passed right over top of those bubbles of TNT.

I posted two men on the bow and told them to lean out over the gunwale and watch the water ahead. In addition, I gave four men binoculars and asked them to keep a peeled eye for enemy boats. The rest of us stood, half upright, half crouched, to keep from being seen.

While we were feeling our way through the channel, giving those mines a once-over-lightly, I talked to Head. The *Tanager* officer back in South Harbor had virtually told me I was a damned fool and would end by getting my men killed. Listening to him had planted a nagging doubt in my mind, and I needed a little unquestioning faith. If Head had let me down, the chances are I would have turned around then and there, but he kicked through.

"Hell, Captain," he said, "I'm only a dumb pharmacist's mate, but I can tell you right now I know we're going to get through. I don't know how I know it: I just know it, that's all."

Having laid his vote on the line, he followed it up with useful information. One of his patients on Fort Hughes had come down from the lookout tower, holding a hand over a wound in his belly, and had told him that a Jap mine sweeper was hiding behind Limbones Island close to Fort Frank off the Cavite shore. When Head told me that, we headed to seaward, to give Limbones a wide berth.

The moon was due to rise about one o'clock and highlight us. It would be just like cruising along through the brightness of Broadway back home on a Saturday night when the shows were letting out. That gave us less than two hours in the comparative safety of darkness, and we couldn't hope to get down the coast very far before the moon hung us on a hook. However, if we discovered that the Japs had lifted their picket line when it did come up, we would try to keep going and put as much distance between ourselves and Corregidor as possible.

A searchlight sliced through the night, and Taylor blurted out, "My God, they've picked us up!" But the source of the light lay behind the horizon and, while it was trained directly over our heads, it was impossible for the men behind it to see us because of the curvature of the earth.

"Don't worry about it!" I told him. "They're good, but they can't see through water."

The Japs fired off two large star shells over Corregidor, illuminating that area brilliantly with a ghastly green light. Head guessed they were looking for boats in South Harbor. If he was right and we had still been there, it would have been the pearly gates for us.

Taylor came up with another idea about those rockets. The Japs had been shelling Caballo for a half-hour, but the barrage had stopped now, and he was sure the green rockets were a signal for the Jap guns to lay off so their army could land.

"They did the same thing this morning when they landed on Monkey Point," Taylor reminded me. "They must be landing on Caballo right now."

We sat there listening to the engine turning over, looking back over our shoulders and wondering how the men we'd left behind were making out.

We still had our four-man lookout watching for Jap ships. Steele, Rankin, and Binkley had X-ray eyes. I had used all of them as lookout men on the *Quail,* and they had constantly picked out planes and identified them before anyone else could see them coming. If a man picks up a plane you don't see and no one else sees and thirty seconds later he's proved right, he doesn't have to bring you a recommendation from his oculist. In addition to these men there were Clarke, Taylor, Head, and myself, but so far we hadn't seen anything.

The moon came up from behind the mountains over the

Cavite shore, looking twice as big and luminous as any moon had ever looked to me previously, and just before it came up there was a short period of moon dawn with greater visibility. In that half-light we saw a Jap destroyer close by to seaward and headed the boat to the southeast, toward shore. As the moon poked up higher we saw a second and third destroyer bracketing the first and patrol boats between the destroyers. By this time we had melted into a background of foliage and were creeping along the shore southward.

We passed inside of what we thought was an islet off Point Fuego, but when we stuck our bow out from behind it the lookouts started tumbling aft through the mess of men and gear and waking up those who were sleeping, to report what they'd seen. Directly ahead of us was another Jap destroyer and more patrol boats than we could count. So I turned the boat around and ducked into a cove. The cove was really two coves, an outer cove and, beyond it, through a narrow neck of water, an inner one.

Two small islets about seventy-five feet high stretched lengthwise between the cove and the sea, almost concealing it. There were several good hiding places with clumps of trees and jutting rocks in there, but the men in the bow taking soundings reported we were in dangerous shoals. After a lot of tricky maneuvering, we decided our best bet was to go out to the little islets, lie up against one of them on the inner side, and catch an hour's sleep. I woke up a half an hour before dawn and sat there chewing over the business of trying to make the beach again.

The light was increasing now, so I called the men. Richardson knuckled his eyes to rub the sleep from them and got the motor going. We upped anchor and headed for a stretch of sandy beach in the northeast part of the cove.

"This time," I told the gang, "we've got to snake her in, no matter what happens. Shoals or no shoals."

Three of the men jumped over the side into shallow water and guided the bow through the coral heads, but owing to weeks of malnutrition they were so feeble that when I told them to get back into the boat they couldn't haul themselves over the side and we had to lift them in. Kicking ahead slowly with the engine, we worked her in and pushed her far enough to run a line from her bow to the beach and tie her up to a tree.

It was a long way from the concealment I had hoped to find, but it was the best we could do. Cucinello drove the men like the warden of a Georgia chain gang, and they started felling trees all over the beach. Where they found the hatchets in the jumble of gear littering the boat I'll never know. I warned them not to cut too many trees near the landing place, since we didn't want it to have a freshly denuded look. Taylor and Steele grabbed the trees as they came aboard and filled the boat with them, arranging them with the trunks downward to achieve the effect of normal growth. It was amazing how many branches and trees it took to cover one small boat. We had her about half covered when Swisher said in his soft Iowa drawl, "Captain, I hear a plane."

The men ashore flopped in the bushes and those in the boat dropped to the floor boards. The alarm caught Meeker and Newquist in the water. They stayed there with their heads under leafy branches, and in a few seconds a plane came down from the north along the coast at a low altitude. We saw it swing left and go over the hills to the southeast.

Out to Sea

With the sound of its motor still beating against our eardrums, we stayed where we were, and a minute or two later the roar increased and the plane skimmed over the hill behind us, swooping down two hundred feet above our heads.

"It's going to strafe us, Captain," Cucinello said. "Gimme an automatic."

But it didn't strafe us. It headed out to sea and went north.

There was no doubt in anybody's mind that they had seen us, and we wanted to get the hell out of there, but there was no use going out in broad daylight. We'd have been picked up in a minute.

"We'll take to the hills if they come for us," I said. "In the meantime half of you keep on camouflaging; the other half take the emergency rations and water ashore."

We finished both jobs and collected behind a thicket of trees among the rocks in a little gully near a ledge of overhanging volcanic stone. The rocks lay thick and jagged, and there was no place to lie down and be comfortable.

There were several ways the Japs could come back and get us. They could run a destroyer in and blast us out with heavy guns. They could come at us in patrol boats and make a landing. They could lay eggs on us from planes, or they could send an expedition at us overland from our rear. One by one we began to eliminate these possibilities. A destroyer without a landing boat wouldn't be dangerous. We'd just move out of the place and back away from the coast. The lip of overhanging rock above us was an ideal protection from a plane. The other two methods of attack were the ones we had to be on our guard against.

Something was chasing itself around in Stringer's mind

and he put it into words. "Captain, do you think the plane really saw us?"

Cucinello was scornful of such naïveté. "How could he help see us?" he asked.

"Seems like if he'd seen us, he'd of circled round to take a good look," Stringer said.

Gradually I had arrived at the same conclusion myself. The Jap had flown directly over us, and there was a chance that we had huddled there beneath him in the one position which was his blind spot.

But the only smart way to play it was to assume that he *had* seen us and make our plans accordingly. I told Cucinello to pick out the men who had had the most sleep, station them as lookouts, and tell all of them to stay out of sight. That warning wasn't needed. When one of them so much as stuck his ears up from behind a bush, the rest of the gang pounced on him and dragged him down.

In spite of the fact that we were playing squat tag with death, the thing had an amusing angle. Here they were, sixteen web-footed sailors, pretending to be scouts crawling along on their hands and knees as if they were sneaking up on a tribe of redskins. At the same time they were making so much noise with their heavy Army-issue shoes that by comparison a herd of buffaloes would have been mouse-quiet and feather-footed.

I forgot to mention that back at Caballo two of our mess boys had come running down the dock just before Head arrived. I had seen them arguing with the *Tanager* officer still standing there and heard them call out to me in despairing voices, "Please, Captain, can't we go with you?"

"I told them they couldn't go with you, Captain," the

Out to Sea

Tanager officer said. "Your boat is already overloaded." I yelled to them to come aboard anyhow. Almost hysterically grateful, they got in and huddled together in practically no space at all.

Now they came up to me and began pouring out their gratitude all over again. I gave them a gentle brush-off by telling them I was busy and not to worry about giving us any more thanks. "Can we go now?" they asked.

I realized they were asking me if it would be all right for them to go home to their families. They were enlisted in the Navy, and there was a question in my mind as to whether I could take it on myself to say it was O.K. for them to take a powder out of the service. Once your mind is grooved Navy fashion it stays grooved even when the ordinary ways of doing things are blowing up all around you. Then I remembered that the *Canopus* officers had released all of their mess boys on the Bataan beach and that Corregidor had apparently let its Filipinos go on the previous day, when boatloads of them headed toward Manila under a flag of truce. These two incidents eased my mind. The fact that the *Canopus* mess boys left on Bataan were all bayoneted by the Japs and their bodies left piled on the beach where they had been put ashore didn't affect my problem. My two boys, I figured, had an even chance to make it, so I told them they could go, but to be careful.

They lived only thirty miles away, in a little village outside Manila, and they promised that whenever the Americans landed an invading force they would report to the naval commander of that force. Khaki was a sure giveaway to the Japs—the Japs themselves wore a kind of jungle green—so we made them take off their clothes and identification tags. Rummaging around, we managed to outfit them in white. One of the mess boys had tattoo marks on his chest which he had stoically let the tattooer's needle jab into his skin because he thought it would make him more American. Now his grandeur was a liability and we warned him not to let anyone see him naked.

They were overcome by emotion. One of them took my hand and wiped tears away from his face with it. "You are so good to me," he said over and over. Before I knew what he was up to, he had given me a roll of a hundred pesos. I shoved it back at him and said, "Your family'll need this." He had four hundred more pesos he said. "You don't have any money, Captain," he insisted. "You will need it more," and much to his joy, I took it. Then they went up the ravine and over the hill.

That was the first time we'd thought about money, but now we checked over our cash and, finding that among us we had between five and six hundred dollars with which to buy food and Diesel oil, we pooled it into a common fund.

It was about time for me to go up on the hill to look around myself; and falling, slipping, and grabbing at shrubs and roots, I set out. By the time I had made it, I was ready for the cleaners. I was readier than that when I saw where we were. We were barely five miles down the coast, and I could still see the tip of Corregidor. All of the preceding night we must have been heading into a current. And, I thought bitterly, if that current had been a little stronger, we might have ended up by backing into South Harbor under the Jap guns.

6

Hide-and-Seek

I CAME back down the hill, chop-fallen and worried, sliding, tearing my hands on thorns. The hills were carpeted with brier thickets growing between hardwood trees eight feet in diameter. In the little valley the growth was matted and impenetrable, but on the hills it was sparser and more like the underbrush back home, although, of course, back home we didn't have mahogany and narrawood trees and iguanas and monkeys rustling in the branches and wild goats leaving droppings around. When I got back with my hide flayed, I was a case for Doc Head, and it took him half an hour to patch me up.

In spite of my dismay at finding ourselves still within spitting distance of a place I'd hoped we'd left behind us, I had taken time to notice that eastward from the hill there were cultivated areas not more than a mile away which sharply limited the area in which we could hide if we had to leave our boat.

My trip had taught me still another unpleasant truth. I was too exhausted to do much scouting. My normal weight was about one hundred and fifty pounds and I was down to about one hundred and thirty. The men were on the rocks physically, too. They could barely get themselves up a hill and certainly they couldn't carry heavy equipment with them.

So when Meeker's first thought was to place us on stringent rations, I set him on a new tack. We broke out the two most nourishing items in our larder, canned beef and tomato juice, and each man had a generous quantity. When it was gone, they were still ravenous, so I told Meeker to dish out a little more of the same. The men tried to get me to eat first, handing me their portions and saying, "This is yours, Captain. We'll get ours later." I put the kibosh on that but I had to watch them to keep them from fattening up my portion at the expense of their own. It happened that way for the next thirty-one days, and I had to check on them like a G-man at every meal to keep them from overfeeding me.

After we had eaten, we tried to stretch out and rest. Our bedding was a few blankets and oilskin khaki ponchos stuck together like sheets of flypaper. We put in a half-hour pulling them apart, and when we lay down we kept reaching under us and groping for small rocks prodding us in the back. Those rocks were as fertile as turtles. No sooner would we pick one out and toss it away than two more took its place. At last fatigue took care of the rock situation, and we slept for four hours like men doped to the eyebrows.

A lookout woke us, tearing down through the brush. He shouted before he reached us that a mine sweeper followed by a whole string of patrol boats was coming from Fortune Island and heading our way. Sleep-groggy, we started to pack our gear and fill our canteens from the water breakers. Each man made up a load, but taking a look at their ribs sticking out and the skin drawn tight over their cheekbones I cut the loads in half.

Peering through the bushes, we could see the mine sweeper, followed by hundred-foot patrol boats. There were sixteen of them, empty and riding high in the water, heading up the shore toward Corregidor. We didn't know what to make of them. Our guess was that they were coastal-type mine sweepers going in to sweep our mines so that their ships could get into Manila Bay.

Anyhow, they didn't come into our cove, so we lay around and talked things over. Haley and Wolslegel said they hoped that they would never be sent back to Honolulu. They just couldn't take it, they said. "Right off the bat we'd get hung for murder. We'd be walking down the street and see a Jap, and it wouldn't make any difference whether we were at peace with them by that time or if the Jap were an American citizen, we'd kill him. We'd know better but we wouldn't be able to help ourselves, and we'd end up in jail sure."

Steele, Newquist, Haley, Meeker, and Bercier were fascinated by the idea of being hunters and worked on me to take them someplace where they could "live off the land," and subsist by hunting and fishing. Sailors always have the cockeyed notion that they would be bear cats on land if only somebody would give them a chance. Maybe it's a throwback to the days when they played cowboys and Indians on stick horses and maybe it's because not knowing much about land operations makes it seem easy to them. And maybe it's just wishful thinking. I let them ramble on. I had a hunch that fate and the Japs would take care of that.

"Tonight," I told them, "we'll drop down the coast about five miles and try to find a place a little closer to the Jap picket boats so we can get an idea of how and when they relax their patrol. But before we do that, the first thing is to lighten our boat and throw out useless gear." Thinking of junk made me remember our loot from the *Ranger*, and I asked Binkley to crawl out onto the boat under the branches and bring me the charts. He came back with the charts but reported that the dynamite and sextant had been left behind on the *Ranger* in the confusion of getting away.

I swallowed hard at the news. Steele had been our general handy man and repair man, our "Mister Fix-it," on the *Quail*. He had proved to be the cleverest one of the crew with a lathe or tools. "It's up to you to make us a sextant out of old razor blades or something," I told him. "We're not going to get very far in the open sea navigating by thumb." Steele said he would start milling it over in his head.

After a while we had chow and lay around letting the good feeling of rest and relaxation flow into our bodies. We could feel it pumping into us like a blood transfusion.

That was the day I sat on the porcelain hand-colored miniature of my wife and two children and smashed it into fifty pieces. I had carried it in my hip pocket all those months, and finding out I had broken it made me feel almost as sunk as discovering we were still in Corregidor's back yard. I didn't throw the pieces away. I made up my mind I'd hang on to them come hell or high water and

Hide-and-Seek

when I got back to civilization I'd have them put together again by an expert.

I had got a radiogram from my wife at the end of December telling me that the family had come through the bombing of Pearl Harbor safely. We had a house back over the hills from the water at Honolulu, and no bombs had come near her. I had left a bunch of written instructions for her to get out of the place if war came, and I had a hunch she hadn't paid any attention to my advice but was still there so that she could at least be in the same part of the world with me and could keep an eye on the home she had put so much care and thought into. I had written to her to push the house down the side of the hill and beat it, but I couldn't advise her further than that because I didn't know how thick Jap subs were between Hawaii and the mainland. From Bataan we couldn't put much in our letters home about ourselves. I remember I wrote, "I'm well and safer than I should be," and that was all the censor would pass.

During the afternoon, the Jap mine sweeper and patrol boats came back past the cove entrance. This time they were loaded with men standing upright and closely packed together. Through our binoculars we could see they were clad only in underdrawers. We counted about a hundred and fifty men to each boat. The total would be about 2400 men. Their faces and bodies were white. They were prisoners from Corregidor, Drum, Frank, and Fort Hughes, being taken in the direction of Fortune Island. We strained our eyes through our glasses, trying to pick out familiar faces. We had the feeling that there but for the grace of God went we. Then that feeling was replaced by the one that before it was all over we might be in an even worse spot than those poor guys sardined together in their skivies.

About three o'clock the sky fell on us. The lookouts came tumbling down with news that Jap soldiers were coming at us from the land side. Swisher and Steele went up to scout the lay of the land. The rest of us put our heads together to plan a defense against a landward invasion. We prepared one based on each end of our strip of beach. And since the Japs were apt to get up on the cliff above us, our answer to that was to send out a group to get behind them, in a strategy of infiltrating the infiltrators.

I sent Wolslegel, Bercier, and Rankin up with automatic rifles to work their way behind the Japs. They came back in five minutes wearing Chessy-cat grins. The invading army of Japs had proved to be natives going out to work in the fields. Swisher's alarm died hard. "Natives, hell," he said, "I heard 'em crawling around in the trees and branches."

"Those were iguanas," Steele said. "I heard 'em too."

From then until dusk our spirits climbed back up the thermometer, and the men amused themselves by walking around barefooted to see if they could toughen up their feet.

After sunset, Watkins and Bercier started to remove the branches from the boat, stripping them from the shore end first to keep us camouflaged toward the sea as long as possible.

The next thing I knew, Taylor, who was on lookout, came hobbling back with the news that a Jap destroyer was around the point and coming fast. The men in the

Hide-and-Seek

boat went back to shore and tried to make themselves part of the bushes and rocks. Fortunately, most of the tree camouflage was still in place, but I had taken a hard look at that camouflage job while I was up on the hill that morning and it wasn't so good. From a few hundred yards away you could make out the shape of a boat with no trouble at all.

Then around the edge of the little islet a gray bow appeared.

Cucinello said it for the rest of us. "If those muzzlers come in here, our goose is cooked."

"What do you suppose they're going to do, Captain?" said Meeker.

I didn't answer. I was trying to dope that one out for myself.

But Steele didn't fool around with useless speculation. "I don't know what they're going to do, but I know what I'm going to do," he announced, and crammed bullet clips into his rifle.

Taylor plucked my arm and said, "They've got their anchoring detail out on the fo'c'sle—they're going to anchor right in here!"

Something had happened to us that was due to happen a lot more times in the days to come. We had been up mentally. Then we had been taken by the scruff of the neck and slammed down again, hard. Once more we felt unsure and hunted and badgered. That peaceful, relaxed feeling we had been sopping up drained away. The rest of our lookouts came downhill from their vantage points but for once they came cautiously, not making any noise at all.

I quit the shallow, fast breathing I was doing and used

the bottom part of my lungs for the first time since the can had stuck its nose in on us. The Jap had its crew lined up at muster quarters just as if they were sailing into Yokohama Harbor in peacetime. Their guns were trained in and their range finders were secured, ready for the night.

They were only five hundred yards away, and it seemed impossible that they couldn't see us and, if not us, our boat. As nearly as we could tell, they were looking straight at us. But they calmly backed their engines and dropped anchor with a rumble of cable in the hawsepipes.

I put Steele and Binkley out at the water's edge to warn us the instant she lowered a boat, and the rest of the gang got the guns set up and ready for a last-ditch battle. I put some of them behind rocks and ledges, with instructions to move over into the ravine alongside the overhanging lip of rock and climb farther up and fan out behind big boulders if the Japs started shelling us with its main battery guns.

I asked Haley, our bos'n's mate with the extra tread of calluses on his feet, how he was doing. "O.K.," he said. "Only I won't be really O.K. until I get my hands on the jerks who pulled that fast one on me back there in the tunnel and stole my bos'n's knife."

By this time it was dusk and the destroyer's outline was growing indistinct. We could hear their blowers dying down. One of her ports was badly closed and a yellow glow was leaking out around it.

Starlight illuminated the bay, but back where we were it was pitch-black. Groping through the bushes, we were six inches away from a white blob before it became a face. Steele and I crawled along, putting a hand on each man in turn and telling them to get together. When we were huddled in a tight group I explained why I didn't think the Japs had seen us. Since they hadn't made any move to lower a boat, the chances were they weren't going to lower one that night. The business of bedding the ship down seemed to be evidence we had been granted a stay of execution. Our only chance as I saw it was to get into the water and pull the boat along the shore and over the reef until we got around the point and into the next cove and start her up there. Somebody suggested that maybe we could use oars, but Haley put the pin on that.

"There aren't any oars," he told us.

I don't know how he knew. The way we had tossed things into the boat when we left the *Ranger*, there could have been a folding elephant in it and I wouldn't have known it. But we took his word for it.

"How about when we get around the point?" someone asked. "Maybe there'll be another Jap can in the next cove."

It was a possibility, but the thing that worried me was the fact that it took a certain amount of know-how to do the job I had suggested.

A coral head is an instrument dreamed up by nature and the devil to punch holes in boat bottoms and tear flesh from unwary bodies. It is a mass of coral—or rock-encrusted coral—and is the nearest thing to an underwater barbed-wire fence there is. "Unless you know what you're doing you're going to be splashing around and making more noise than six motors," I told them. "Almost none of you can swim, and you're going to have to hang onto the boat half the time when you're passing over holes in the cove bottom to keep from drowning." Then I asked myself what we would do if the Japs heard us and turned a searchlight on us when we were halfway around the point. The more I thought about the plan, the worse it seemed.

I thought maybe a little prodding would stir up something workable, so I gave out a prod.

"I can always take you to Nasugbu," I said.

"Where's that?" Cucinello wanted to know.

"A little town about ten miles down the coast, out of the fighting zone. There's a Jap garrison there made up of home-guard troops, and there's a fair chance they'll take us in and not shoot us. We can leave all of our equipment here, and I can hike you over the hills and we can go into Nasugbu in the morning with our hands up."

There was a pause. Then Steele said, "If you'll let us take our guns, I'm all for it. If I go in that dump I want to go in shooting." About a dozen more piped up and said, "And how." Their voices were so loud I said, "For Christ's sake, pipe down. Do you want to wake up the whole Jap navy?"

But the prod brought forth a suggestion from Head. "I'm only a dumb pharmacist's mate," he began again, "but it looks to me as if we'd drape some more camouflage around that boat and stick it out here until morning we won't be any worse off than we are right now. We can see what we're doing then, and that Jap may haul up her anchor and leave at daybreak."

Somebody wanted to know how an old guy with a gray thatch like his had ever managed to come up with such a bright idea. "Listen," he told us, "I'm the youngest man in the party." He was in his forties, and we had kidded him

Hide-and-Seek

about his hardening arteries and second childhood, and he had whipped out a few fast ones about the rest of us being wet behind the ears and our voices still changing. But grayheaded or not, he had been smart enough to cut through the fog and put his finger on a solution. Since that Jap can had sneaked in at twilight, it was likely she didn't want to be seen any more than we did, was in there for concealment just as we were, and would sneak out again in the morning. I remembered that the Jap mine sweeper we had seen riding herd on the prison boats that afternoon had all its guns pointed at the sky, as if it were uneasy about an air attack, and if our Jap destroyer shared that fear it meant she wouldn't want to be caught sitting there in a cove during daylight.

About midnight we put some more branches around the edge of the boat. When that chore was done, Steele, not being satisfied with merely trying to get away with his life, began to think up things he wanted to do to the Jap. "If we could only find that dynamite," he muttered, "and if I only had some fuses, I'd swim out to that can and give her a touching up."

It was a fine idea, I told him, if we had dynamite, which we hadn't brought with us, and if he could swim, which he couldn't.

He refused to be downed. "You give me a life jacket like you did going out to do the scuttling and I can swim," he said.

"If you find some dynamite, I'll decide later," I told him, thinking if he found it we could at least fix it so he wouldn't have to bear the brunt of the expedition alone.

In the meantime, we tied on more branches close to the water line and stopped stumbling and smashing our faces against rocks.

About two o'clock the moon came up and we moved farther back into the bushes. With the first streaks of dawn, I watched the Jap destroyer. One thing we had noticed about the Japs. It had never ceased to surprise us all through the war—they didn't like to get up early in the morning. They'd send out one scout plane promptly enough, but the other planes wouldn't show until around nine o'clock. We discovered the Jap navy lay late abed, too. After a while the sunrays shot higher in the sky and began to light up the mountain peaks. The destroyer began to show signs of life. She went about the business of getting under way leisurely, and if ships could have yawned and stretched, that Jap can would have done it. She lifted her anchor, backed and filled a few times, and headed out to sea. For the first time since we'd seen her, we stopped whispering and began to talk normally once more.

During the course of the morning I asked Taylor how his leg was. The doctor had told him that if he got it wet with salt water, gangrene would set in, and scuttling the *Quail* had given it a good soaking. But when we looked at it, the ugly-looking sores seemed better and healthier than before their immersion in brine. Having had visions of Taylor being a stretcher case before we had gone very far, Head and I were encouraged.

We posted lookouts once more and about eight o'clock they reported that the mine sweeper and prison boats were coming back again.

Stringer said wistfully, "If we had a PT boat right now

Hide-and-Seek

we'd be out of here and gone in no time at all and maybe we could give that mine sweeper the old one-two punch so those guys they've corralled could bust loose and get themselves good and lost in the hills."

Richardson wasn't losing any sleep over our lack of a PT. "PT's are all right," he said, "but this engine of ours will take us where we're going if we give it enough time."

We tried to stock up on sleep again, but this time the rocks under the ponchos wouldn't let us get any rest at all. We lay on them, shifting constantly and looking up through the trees at a patch of sky.

About eleven o'clock the mine sweeper and the patrol boats returned, once more loaded down with prisoners. After that there were no more patrol boats.

How to break through the Jap patrol line was a problem I had kicked around in my mind so much it was worn smooth and I couldn't get a good grip on it any more, so I asked the men if they had any ideas on the subject. None of them had anything to offer except Wolslegel, who suggested heading out to sea. They didn't seem very worried about it. You could see they thought it was my baby and it was up to me to change its didies.

After sunset we were making preparations to get under way and dragging our supplies down to the water's edge when the lookout from the westward point came in tight-lipped. "That damned Jap can is coming back again," he told us.

Sure enough, in the gap between the islet and the end of the point a gray prow appeared cutting through the water. Cucinello and Taylor were cursing and banging their fists against rocks in rage and bitter disappointment. The bow disappeared behind the islet. Then the midship torpedo section and finally the stacks and the stern slid by. We waited for her to reappear on the other side of the islet and either turn in or not turn in, our bodies arched with the intensity of our concentration. We saw her go on by without turning and head in the next cove to the south.

That was a signal for action. Everybody made a rush for the boat. We tossed out most of the trees and branches, leaving only the ones tied along the sides.

Richardson started the engine, and we turned around and headed out. It began to look as if we were going to leave that place after all. We had begun to think we would still be there putting trees on the boat and taking them off when we were old men.

Clouds covered the sky and there was no starlight. We couldn't have planned that blackout better if we had been standing by the switch in the sky where they turned the illumination on. Tuckered out by stiff climbing and emotional acrobatics, the crew turned in and were asleep by the time we had cleared the cove.

We headed straight out to give the Jap in the next cove elbowroom and then turned south along the coast. Our plan was to try to make a break through the picket line between Fortune Island and Nasugbu, and if we couldn't make it through there, to try the longer route outside of Fortune. And we went over the night and the sea with our eyes trying to see everything there was to see, squinting in the darkness as if we were looking into the noonday sun. A white light flashed on, close aboard, high and above us. It blinked several times and was followed by another light to the left, blinking dots and dashes.

Hide-and-Seek

It snapped off, and Taylor asked, "Do you see what I see?"

I saw them all right. Three Jap destroyers were passing us on our seaward side. I headed closer to shore, and the three Japs came past us with their high-speed blowers whee-e-e-ing in our ears. They swept on down the sea lane, using their blinkers at frequent intervals like maneuvering signals, or lights operated by a sound screen listening with electrical ears for subs. We stayed close in, so that any echo they got from us would be scrambled by the echoes they got from the beach.

They kept on until they vanished to the south. It seemed to me a good place for us would be right in behind them, like a halfback following his interference through a screen of tacklers, so I headed back out to tag along in their wake. We trailed them for about a thousand yards, when our interference let us down. There, heading across our course to the shore, was still another Jap can.

We were on a collision course with this one and certain to bump into it unless we moved quickly. I gave the boat a hard rudder and spun her around. The Jap cleared us by a few hundred yards—the distance was anybody's guess in the dark. She was close enough so we could hear sounds coming from her machinery. Then she went pounding on by into a cove south of us.

Just when I was expecting another one to drop down out of the sky and sit in our laps, I had an idea. There must be a hole in the picket line where those babies had come from, and our best bet was to go hell-bent for that hole before they sent more cans out there to plug it up. If I could find it, it would be an empty pocket in the night with nothing in it for the moment.

The area to the north of Fortune seemed clear of ships. Between Fortune and the beach, patrol boats were clustered at close intervals, but outside toward the sea the intervals between them were greater. A half mile from the western edge of Fortune I could see one of the boats on its regular beat headed toward Fortune before turning round to make the other leg of its run in the other direction. We waited for it to complete its eastward run, and as it headed westward we made our dash. We went quite close to Fortune—possibly only two hundred yards away.

I figured the Japs would have sentries all around that island, walking guard on the men we had seen them herding along in patrol boats behind the mine sweeper. I couldn't see how those sentries could help seeing us. But I was banking on their thinking we were one of their own patrol boats, and apparently that was what happened, for no alarms were raised.

By this time it seemed nothing could make us feel any queerer than the things that had already happened to us, but sliding through that water, knowing that within a long golf drive of us were thousands of men who had wanted to get away just as badly as we (but hadn't got the breaks we had—so far), was queerer than anything that had gone before. I wondered if Pete Welch was sitting on his haunches somewhere up there peering in our direction, or McCracken or Colonel Foster. Only I didn't think any of them would be on Fortune. Probably the Japs had taken the officers to Japan to display them, like Roman conquerors. Still, you couldn't tell.

Hide-and-Seek

I made myself think about the boat. Once past Fortune, we shifted our course back to the Luzon coastline. I started worrying about the moon and began to get the itch for more speed. We had been running on half throttle to keep down the noise of our engine, but now I told Richardson to open her up and give her the gun. All she would take.

I told Taylor to go forward and see if he could find anything to throw out we hadn't already thrown overboard. Even with that it didn't seem as if we could be making more than four knots. Taylor dropped the Lewis machine guns overboard. They were heavy, and we had more guns than we knew what to do with. He also tossed out a number of small mushroom anchors we had used in mine sweeping. And we lost sight of the patrol boats northward.

7

Helping Hands

WE WERE out where there are no landmarks. There were no stars to steer by, and we didn't dare turn on a light to see the compass. All we could do was put Fortune Island on our stern, keep it there, and head for the mainland. I had picked out a spot on the chart down on the Kalatayan peninsula where there was a little island just off the beach. The chart showed two fathoms of water around it, and back in the cove we'd stopped in I'd promised the boys we'd put up alongside the beach, camouflage her again, and let them get the gear sorted out. Shipshape was more than just a phrase to them. The jumbled mass of junk under their feet was driving them crazy.

We spotted our island all right, but when we were still a mile from the beach we saw breakers ahead and couldn't locate the opening the chart had indicated. After cruising back and forth for an hour we anchored just outside of the breakers, to wait for morning.

Using an oarlock as a weight, Binkley had made a lead line for taking soundings, and at dawn we started all over again, hunting for the opening in the long, low, flat reef,

Helping Hands

taking great care our propeller didn't graze anything. By the time we had made our third attempt, the sun had come up and we could see the tops of masts just over the horizon off to the north and west.

A plane might be along any time, and knowing we couldn't just sit there dumb and helpless all day staring at that reef we headed south, hoping the foam kicked up by the surf would make us hard to see from a distance.

When we saw the Cape Santiago lighthouse sticking its long neck up over the horizon to the south we worked our way in to about fifty yards from the beach and anchored. Looking at that beach and not being able to reach it, we felt like kids with their noses flattened against a candy-store window, but brooding about it wasn't any good, so we did the best we could.

First we unscrewed the brass taffrail which rose up four feet from our stern and threw it overboard. Then we decided that if anything came near, all the men would get down out of sight except one man and myself, who would smear dirty oil from the bilge over our faces, arms, and legs. By this time the sun had burned all the clouds out of the sky and it was getting hot. We had thrown away our tin helmets even before we'd left Corregidor. They would have been no good against the sun anyhow. In that glare they would only have served as fireless cookers for our brains.

At Corregidor, working mostly at night and sleeping by day, we had lost the tan we'd got earlier in the war. We were pale as ghosts and a pushover for the sun's rays, so we put our khaki ponchos across the boat and crawled under. It was even hotter under there than out in the open, but while we might come out feeling like steamed clams we wouldn't get our shells all sunburned. We lay there with the sweat rolling from us and couldn't sleep. Inevitably our minds began to focus on drinking water. We had a good supply, enough to allow each man one canteenful each day, and we declared the daily dividend then and there. It would have been much better if we had suffered for a while and put off our drinks until later in the afternoon, for after the first blissful gulp gurgled down our gullets, our mucous membranes started drying up again and we were thirstier than before.

In the afternoon I broke out the charts and made our plans for the night. The southwest monsoon was coming up from seaward. It was getting rougher by the minute, and I wanted to get inside the ring of the islands for protection. We were now about forty miles from Corregidor and figured on chalking up fifty more miles before the next morning. Our third stop was supposed to be Malacaban Island in the Verde Island Passage. Richardson had been pressing me for a chance to overhaul the engine before we tried any long jumps, and I figured if Malacaban provided good concealment we'd lay over there and let him work on it before it broke down one day when the Japs were about to hop us.

About one o'clock we sighted heavy bombers high above us whipping out of Manila and heading south in a hurry. We found out later the Coral Sea battle had been fought and lost by the Japs only the day before. Those planes must have been replacements going out too late to do any good.

It had been so hot that I had let the men lower themselves over the side a few times. While the salt water was evaporating from their clothes and bodies it made them cooler for an hour or so. It was a long, rolling, pitching, prickly hot, worrisome, intolerable day, but night came down at last and at eight o'clock it was dark enough to get under way. In about half an hour Richardson discovered that the engine was spitting oil. We covered it with canvas and looked it over by flashlight. Oil was leaking through the crankcase, but there was nothing we could do about it except refill the tank periodically partly with new oil and partly with oil skimmed up from the bilge pocket. Richardson said he could keep it going if we'd stop the engine every now and then to salvage the wasted oil and pour it back in again.

"Stop it—how often?" I asked.

He couldn't tell. It might be every four hours, or it might be as often as every half-hour. It wouldn't take very long each time . . . only a matter of minutes.

About a mile from the island we began to see what looked like a whole fleet blocking our path between Malacaban and the Luzon mainland. We swung south to go through the Verde Island Passage. There were two Jap patrol boats parked in the passage ahead and two more—one on either side of us. However, they were well apart from each other —about two thousand yards. And we went crawling in there between them through the passage. As we reached a point abeam of the eastern end of Malacaban, we saw two more Jap patrol boats. The little headway we had been making was now reduced to nothing. We were caught in a strong tidal current running through the passage against us like a millrace. We knew that six hours after the current started to run against us it would turn around and start to run the other way, but we didn't know whether that switch would take place in five hours or five minutes. Meanwhile we just about managed to hold our own, which meant that we were motionless. Held there helpless, we saw two destroyers nestled against the south-central beach and two of the largest subs I'd ever seen, about the size of our own sub *Argonaut*. We could hear them charging their storage batteries, which helped drown out the sound of our own engine.

Racing madly ahead without moving an inch, like men in a nightmare trying to run in wet concrete, we remained there for three hours. The crew slept peacefully, and Taylor and myself were both so groggy that even as I held onto the tiller in a half-sitting, half-standing posture I found myself slumping down into the engine pit, asleep, then coming out of it and pulling myself back up.

I tried whipping myself with a lash of self-administered fight talk. "Here you are," I said to myself, "bang in the middle of one of the most dangerous moments of your life and you're falling asleep like a big dope." But the steady drone of the engine and the fact that although much might happen nothing was actually happening at the moment sent me off again. After one of my periodic falls into the engine pit I noticed we were making a little progress, and I said to Taylor, "Don't look now, Guns, but I think we're actually moving." We had gained about a hundred yards on those two patrol boats on each side of us, when Stringer announced that the engine was out of oil.

"Can't you keep her going a few minutes more?" I begged him.

He shook his head. "She'll burn up," he said.

Helping Hands

So we stopped, and watched ourselves drift back through the first line of patrol boats and then on back through the second line. Richardson and Stringer were working like fiends under the canvas with a flashlight while Taylor and I held its edges down to keep even a pinprick of radiance from showing. They soon had it refilled again and started the engine. By this time the current had turned and was on our side, and we came charging back past those two lines of picket boats and sped out into clear water, changing our course to get back to the Luzon mainland.

With the current we were making about eight knots. But just as we entered the north channel, a light flashed on, on the edge of the beach toward Verde Island, and immediately opposite it on the Luzon coast another light appeared, both of them low down and near the water's edge. We were exactly between them. "What goes on?" I asked Taylor. He thought they were just a couple of fishing-boat lights, but the lights moved along their respective beaches keeping us always exactly between them as we continued through the passage. "These birds have got some kind of sound gear," I told Guns. "They're tracking us."

"If that's so, why don't they do something about it?" he wanted to know.

I couldn't tell, unless it was because our boat had such a shallow draft and was so small that they didn't quite know whether they had picked up a boat or a drifting mahogany log and were unable to hear us properly.

Stringer allowed the engine down to bare steerageway so that whatever they'd been hearing before they'd hear less of now, and it wasn't very long before the two lights reversed their direction and went back up the beach so fast they looked like tracer bullets. It was as if they had come to the end of a track on which they had been running and a trick mechanical device had zoomed them back to their starting places to pick up something they could really get their hooks into.

At three-thirty, as we headed up the coast to round Point Punas, the moon climbed over the horizon. It was like coming out of a dark tunnel into broad daylight and it would have been lovely if we had been out on a week-end fishing cruise. I had hold of the tiller and stood there swaying back and forth with the pressure of the water against it. Looking ahead, I noticed that we were entering a moonlit river with high trees on each side. On one of these trees was a farmhouse and a windmill perched on its topmost limb. Trying to think what a house was doing on top of a tree, I shook my head so I could see it more clearly and it was gone. The river had gone too. There was nothing there but the broad open water and the bay.

"Guns," I said, "I'm a little pooped. You take the tiller. Keep that high peak over there on your port bow and give me a call in about half an hour."

I curled up around his feet and went to sleep on the after-taffrail deck. He must have let me sleep for a lot more than half an hour. When he woke me dawn was breaking and we were well up the coast.

"I would have let you sleep longer," he explained, "but I was beginning to see things that weren't there. I saw breakers right ahead of us and I was about to turn around to avoid 'em when all of a sudden they weren't there any more, so I figured I'd better do something about it before I mistook a Jap cruiser for San Diego Harbor."

"Me too," I told him, "only my specialty was farmhouses and windmills." But Taylor was snoring even before I finished the sentence. I asked Binkley for the charts, and we started looking for a river so we could replenish our fresh water. We picked out one as far away from a town as possible and made for it. When we hit it we noticed a few native houses scattered near by and, thinking that the natives might be a source of danger, we went on beyond the spot to a likely-looking beach where a jutting point of land thrust a finger of trees out along the shore. We eased the boat in and tied her up, and no sooner had we finished than a group of natives came walking down the beach toward us.

We had had glowing accounts of Filipino loyalty from our Army, and we'd heard from our own Navy people about the exceptional quality of the Filipino scouts. We hoped that the ones we ran into would be O.K., but we knew also that the Jap heel when placed on a conquered neck is a grinding affair with hobnails and spikes in it. We also knew that if any native or group of natives dared to help us they would be signing their own death warrants right then and there if the Japs ever found out about it. So whether or not any of them would have the guts to give us a lift with shelter and food after Corregidor fell was a question mark in our minds. At least that was the way I felt about it. The men worked it out much simpler than that. If they knew the Filipinos they trusted them. If they hadn't been in the islands long enough to know them, they kept their fingers crossed.

These particular ones came slowly at first but as soon as they were near enough to see we had white faces they came running lickety-split. Meeker, Cucinello, and Head jumped off the boat to meet them. The Filipinos started the conversation with a torrent of English, talking so fast we couldn't understand a word. As soon as the torrent of words dammed itself enough for us to make out what they were saying, they asked us, "We hear on Jap radio Corregidor has fallen." Shrugging apologetically they added, "But we know Japs always lie." They waited for us to tell them it wasn't true. There was an embarrassed silence from us, but there was no point in denying what they were sure to discover for themselves sooner or later. So we admitted Corregidor was gone and asked them if there were any Japs near by.

"No Japs have been here," they said. "At next village about ten kilometers away there are a few Japs."

"This place is no good to hide," an older man said. "We will show you a better place." It brought us up short, but now was as good a time as any to put the natives to a test, and we decided to take a chance and see what would come of it. They unfastened the boat lines for us and, half swimming and half walking on the sandy bottom, they towed us down the beach a half mile where there was an indentation in the coastline from which a small fresh-water stream flowed. They beached the boat for us where overhanging trees and projecting rocks formed a natural covering and we wouldn't need further camouflaging.

We dragged cans and water breakers ashore, and Meeker started breakfast.

I got hold of the village schoolteacher and questioned him about the location of the Jap garrisons in the various

Helping Hands

parts of the islands. One by one we checked off the places to steer shy of.

After Meeker got breakfast ready, we offered food to the Filipinos but, seeing how little we had, they refused to take it. Some of the older ones shouted words in Tagalog to the small boys, and shortly afterward a large assortment of fruit and vegetables appeared. We offered to pay for them, but the natives merely smiled and said nothing. Meeker asked them if they knew any place where we could buy rice and chickens, and they explained that there was almost no rice in the province. Hoping to hurt the Jap cause, the farmers had refused to grow it that spring. But they went on to say that they knew where there was one bag of rice in a storehouse some miles away and would get it for us.

I called Meeker, Taylor, and Cucinello into a huddle. "Last night Mr. Taylor and I were so whipped down we weren't making any sense, we were seeing things," I told Cucinello. "So hereafter you'll take charge in the daytime. See that Meeker gets all of the food he wants and that the work is done on the boat while Mr. Taylor and I are sleeping. Right now, call the boys together. I've got something I want to tell them and then you'll be on your own."

When they gathered around, I said, "We've been lucky enough to find the Filipinos both friendly and loyal. From now on, we'll probably meet natives here and there on this trip and I know you won't have any trouble getting along with them, providing one thing—you don't fool with their women. I know you've got too much on your minds to get hot pants, but even just talking to them is liable to arouse jealousy and bad feeling, and it's better to avoid them as far as possible."

Haley supplemented my speech with one of his own. "If one of you guys even so much as bats an eye at a gal between now and when we get where we're going, I'll bash your God-damned heads in," he promised.

There were no dissenting voices. That done, Taylor, Steele, Binkley, and I stretched ponchos in the shade of the coconut trees and slept.

At three o'clock in the afternoon the sound of voices and the sting of biting ants aroused us. The place looked like a truck farmer's pipe dream. We were surrounded by piles of coconuts, bananas, vegetables, and glossy queer fruit. Beside us was a large earthen jug filled with rice. There was ten times as much gathered there as we could eat or get into our boat. Meeker was bending over a steaming pot stewing chickens. We went after that chicken and polished it off along with boiled rice, bananas, coconut milk, coconut meat, and a kind of potato called *camote*. With the wrinkles pushed out of our bellies, we sat around glassy-eyed and full.

Watching us eat, our hosts must have noticed that we had no mess gear such as cups or plates, for they dragged bamboo trees and coconuts down to the beach, cut sections of the trees, and fashioned us a complete set of tumblers. That done, they made us a set of bowls out of coconut shells. They worked magic on bamboo shavings and transformed them into spoons. The work varied, depending on the man who did it. Some of the stuff was beautifully made and some much cruder, but we weren't captious.

Helping Hands

After the meal, the natives showed us a waterfall and filled our breakers. The water was sparkling and tangy, but Head gave it a shot of iodine anyhow, just to make sure. Lazy and full, we walked over to a little pool and took a bath. The natives gave us some coconut soap which made a thin lather, and the men washed their clothes.

When darkness fell, we got into the boat and headed east. The power of that feast was still upon us, weighing down our eyelids, and talk ran slow. With what talk there was, we spoke of how superior these natives were to the drugstore cowboys we were used to seeing around Manila. These were provincial Filipinos.

Sunrise caught us off the northeastern shore of Marinduque, but we kept on toward the south.

Taking a good look at several spots along the coast, we selected one. With the exception of one badly frightened old man we found hiding in a house, the natives had taken to the hills. The whites of his eyes showed and his face was the putty color of fear. We tried to question him, but he was old and didn't speak English very well. While we were talking to him, the younger men came down from the hills. Among them was a United States-trained schoolteacher who explained their fright by saying they had thought we were Japanese. That province had been the center of the Sakdalista, an anti-American, pro-Japanese, prewar revolutionist group. After the Sakdalistas had seen the Japs kick and beat their people and abuse their women, all except a very few had done a political flip-flop and become anti-Japanese.

"How about the few who are still pro-Japanese?" I asked him.

He said simply, "They are all dead. We kill them."

During this talk Richardson was all impatience and when it was over he went to work on me again to give him enough time to overhaul the engine. I told him to go ahead and do his stuff, and we landed our food and pitched camp. Taylor and I went to sleep while the engineers went at the engine with a determined glint in their eyes. By sunset the glint had changed to a worried frown. They reported that the further they went the worse it looked. They figured they were going to have to strip that baby almost down to the bed plates. According to Richardson, it was a miracle it had run thus far. One piston was so badly adjusted it was striking the underside of the cylinder head. It was a wonder we hadn't cracked the cylinder head itself.

I was willing to do anything to keep that piece of mechanism happy and contented—and I said we'd have to take the delay and like it.

Meanwhile Head had been out charging around. In his role of self-appointed public-relations counselor he had made friends with a Filipino who had been a local radio operator before the war and also got chummy with several farmers and plantation owners in the vicinity. There were many friendly callers that evening, and we were offered places to sleep in their homes. They explained that there was a type of insect on the ground that would eat the men alive if they tried to sleep outside protected only by their ponchos.

One of the natives, more prosperous than the rest, asked us to use his guesthouse. The floor was made of split bamboo with cracks between them. On this surface was laid a thick layer of dried palm fronds and above that a light muslin spread. Some of us took him up on his invitation. Others who didn't think much of the floor-sleeping idea spread out their ponchos on the long tables and solid wooden benches. The few who tried getting their sleep native fashion found that their hosts knew a lot more about sleeping in the tropics than we did. It was a steamy, breathless night. Those who slept on muslin and palm fronds were kept cool and comfortable by the circulation of air coming up through the split bamboo. The rest of us tossed restlessly in pools of sweat.

The next day Richardson, Steele, Swisher, and Stringer worked in the blazing sun all day long. They lifted the engine casing off the bed plates, jacked it around, and renewed parts, washers, and gaskets, grimly determined that when they finished with it the engine would be almost as good as new.

In the middle of the morning the son of a wealthy Filipino landowner rode up and said that his father would like to have Head and myself take lunch with him. He led the way through winding trails and mile and after mile of coconut groves while Head and I followed him. We came at last to a hilltop home where we were greeted by a distinguished old gentleman. He led us up the steps of a ranch house that would have fitted perfectly into a California landscape. It was built of timber and had American-style plastered walls.

We sat on the veranda while two of his daughters brought out glasses of chilled coconut milk with the white, soft pulp of the coconut mashed in it.

He apologized for not having it iced, but he had only a few gallons of Diesel oil left for his power plant and was saving it for emergencies. We asked him if he had any extra lubricating oil and offered to buy any he could spare. He said he did have a little he had earmarked for his tractor but probably the Japs would come and take the tractor, anyway, and he would be glad to let us have it.

When lunch was ready we sat down to an elaborate meal. There were many kinds of fish, pork, and rice served in different styles. In deference to a tradition left over from Spanish occupation, only we men ate. The daughters waited on table and one of them operated a hand-powered fan.

Afterward we went back to the veranda. Our host pointed to his tractor, and mentioned the modern conveniences with which he had been blessed under American occupation, such as plumbing, a water system, electric lights, irrigation.

"The Japs might be smart enough to leave you unmolested so you can produce food for them," I suggested.

"When the Japs come they take everything," he said. "Our home was in Manila, and we know. They will take the tractor and the plows, the electric wires, the pumps, even the machetes. We will have to work with stone tools. In Manila, the Japs tore down whole buildings to get steel and send it away to Japan. They take all automobiles and break them up for steel. My son was there and will tell you. He stayed in Manila for a while after the Japs came."

We perked up and got interested.

"How about food in Manila?" we asked the son. He was a grave young man with a face that had forgotten about smiling. He spoke with passionate intensity.

"Outside Manila there is food, inside Manila no. But the worst is not the food. I have been in my friends' homes,

Helping Hands

and Japanese officers will come to door and you must bow. Everybody must bow. Men, women, old ladies, children. If you do not they put you in jail. What they do to you in jail I do not know.

"If Jap officer see a pretty Filipino girl, next day more officers will come and say, 'This house is about to be honored. An officer is about to confer the favor of sharing his blood with one of the Oriental subraces.' But we are Christians and their marriage is not a marriage with us. It is fake marriage, not even real Japanese marriage. Maybe Filipino girl be only temporary wife.

"For your American people it is worse," he went on. "We wept the day the Japs come to Manila. They tie your women and children together and drive them through the streets. Why they do that I do not know. They were not animals. The Japs are bad people. They kick us with their feet and we are not used to it. We are proud, and it makes us angry and we hate them."

We sat there feeling impotent and packed tight with a hard, cold anger. Head was breathing fast through his nose, like a man running.

"What became of the Americans?" we wanted to know.

"They took them to Santo Tomas College. Now a few the Japs have let out. Some very old ladies and some ladies with small children. Japanese bring many geisha girls from Japan. The American ladies must be servant to geisha girls. But they have enough to eat. Maybe it is better for their children to be out of Santo Tomas even so."

Our host broke out two cans of warm beer, but I didn't feel like drinking.

We thanked him and started back to the beach. He went with us part of the way.

"If you stay over until tomorrow I have my men make a mast for you and rig it," he said. "My cooks can feed you and you can rest. In the morning I will send men to your boat. There is a place where you can move it in behind big trees growing out in the water."

We wanted to keep moving. Staying in one spot made us jumpy. Trading another delay for a mast might be a bad bargain, so I told him I wanted to think it over.

"I send my boys down at high water tomorrow, anyhow," he said.

When we got back to the beach, Taylor and Weinmann came to meet us. Taylor was excited.

"I've got some bad news," he said. "About an hour ago a trader's banca put in here. I went out to meet the two Filipinos in it, and bought a Manila newspaper from them."

He showed it to us. On the front page was a photograph of General Wainwright and another American officer standing in front of a table. Sitting about four feet away from them was a sneering Jap officer in an immaculate suit of tropical white. The paper was a Jap-controlled Manila sheet printed in English.

Featured in its main news column was a speech supposed to have been delivered by General Wainwright over the radio. He was reported to have said:

"By the authority vested in me by the President of the United States I hereby reassume command of all Filipino-American forces in the Philippine Islands and I hereby direct the commanding officers of the forces in Mindanao, Leyte, Negros, Samar, and all others in the Philippine Is-

Helping Hands

lands to lay down their arms and surrender as directed by the Imperial Japanese Army. You will understand that in issuing this order I have no other choice."

These may not be the exact words but that was the way I remember them.

There, in a square block on the front page, was a warning that all Filipino and American soldiers, sailors, and officers must surrender themselves at certain listed surrender points prior to noon on May 12, after which the Imperial Army would not accept their surrender.

I said, "What the hell about it?"

But Taylor was hag-ridden by pessimism. "They'll be looking for people like us with a butterfly net, starting tomorrow noon," he said gloomily.

For some reason, having the distant bay of the Jap bloodhounds brought closer by that newspaper made me stubborn and balky. I decided we'd take time out to have a mast made for the boat regardless of bloodhounds and butterfly nets. "Keep your shirt on," I told Taylor. "Tomorrow noon is going to be just like any other day to us."

I explained the situation to the rest of the boys and showed them the newspaper. I told them about the mast and said I wasn't sure we'd be able to get one anywhere else and that in spite of the mechanical savvy they had shown in unraveling the engine and putting it back together again with no pieces left over, it might conk out on us somewhere along the way. If it did a mast would be useful.

I also let them in on the information I had picked up from my planter host that guerrilla fighting was still going on in the Camarines. My guess was the Japs would put a quick end to that, now that they had control of the rest of the islands. I said that any plan we had had of going to Mindanao was out now because it had been surrendered. "From now on," I told them, "we are just eighteen guys hell-bent for Australia by way of the Philippines and Dutch East Indies."

The four engineers were pretty done up. We would let them rest up for another day while our bighearted native friend put in a mast, a boom, and rigging for us. We would get together what food we could. Then we would climb into the boat and sleep there, holding ourselves ready to get under way on an instant's notice.

For the evening meal, the natives had brought in even larger quantities of food. They had cooked several chickens, roasted a pig, killed a calf, roasted that, and were drying meat for us in the sun, although it wouldn't be properly dried until tomorrow.

We got our gear back in the boat and discovered we would have to do something constructive about keeping the ants away from the meat. The natives suggested building a fire with wet wood so that the smoke would blow antward. Meeker and Newquist were appointed to keep the smudge going, while the rest of us slept in the boat. When we were all curled up and fitted together for the night it was impossible for anyone to walk without stepping on somebody else. But we were getting used to sleeping twisted around corners and in pretzel shapes.

There's an art in sleeping on a bare floor or deck. When you get used to it, no feather bed is more comfortable. Taylor and I slept on the taffrail deck, bent around the bollards in a solid comfort we have never matched before or since. The trick is to get the fleshy part of the body to make contact with the boards instead of your bones. For example, it's a good idea to shift and turn until you collect a roll of fat as a pad between your ribs and the sleeping surface. If you put your cheekbone against the boards, you can't stand it for very long at a time, but if the fleshy part of your face is shoved up to insulate the cheekbone you can rest with no trouble at all. When you once get on to it you can get all coiled up so there's no bone touching anywhere. It's tough if you're skinny, but with diligence and application it can still be done.

At dawn, the Filipino boy from the ranch came splashing out to wake us up, his brown legs shooting up showers of diamonds in the new dawn. He pointed out the place down the beach his father had selected for us, and a cloud of chattering Filipino boys helped us work the boat over the reef and berth it behind a grove of mangrove trees with their roots standing spraddle-legged in a lagoon.

When the old patriarch had left Manila he had brought with him everybody who had ever worked for him. Now he turned these retainers loose on our problem and took all of our men ashore to a tenant house where his women were cooking breakfast for us. Off in the jungle was a clear pool of water where the men could bathe. They had done more bathing in the past two days than they had for months. They had had so many layers of dust and grime ground into them back at Corregidor that, as Newquist said, "So far we haven't even gotten through the topsoil."

They weren't very happy about the native women watching them at their ablutions and commenting upon the whiteness of their skin. When they felt liquid feminine eyes resting upon them they grabbed up a towel or pair of shorts and held them before themselves as shy as schoolboys.

"How do we know what they're saying about us in that goofy double talk?" Clarke said. "Haven't they had any bringing up?"

Meanwhile the Filipinos went to work on the mast and the rigging. Carpenters were binding three bamboo trees together with rattan.

The old gentleman's son showed up once more and said that his father would like to have Taylor, Head, and myself as his guests for the day.

There was the same elaborate ceremony. Only this time the girls of the family persuaded their father to ask us to shave. We declined, but the girls insisted and brought us a pan of water, some coconut soap, and an ancient razor with its edges almost rusted away. To make it easier the water was stone-cold. Head gave me a despairing look as if he were saying silently, "The things I do for you and the rest of the gang," and hacked away at his whiskers, his face etched with agony. Halfway through he tried to call the whole thing off. But the girls clapped their hands and said, "*Take it off*," like a strip-tease audience with the sexes reversed. When Head was through I started in on my own private jungle. Every whack of the razor pulled hairs out by the roots. It was a major operation and my nude face felt raw.

When Taylor had endured his trial by cold water and dull steel, the girls said, "Now you look like young men. Before you were very old." We felt our flayed chops ruefully and forced a society grin.

Helping Hands

As a parting gift the old patriarch brought out his only remaining two cigars. He had kept them in an iron safe, packed with a bit of damp sponge. Taylor took one but I turned the other one down. It was the least I could do for him.

Back at the boat I found that the workmen had the mast completed. They carried it to the boat and prepared halyards and stays. By that time our boys had cut out sails, making them from the awnings we had kept to cover the oil drums. We shook hands all around, and at high water the natives worked the boat back over the reef.

Instead of going eastward of Masbate, which was the shortest route, I decided to go west of it through the Sibuyan Sea. There was much shoal water and many reefs and obstructions in the Sibuyan Sea. No good-sized ship would venture through, unless, as in our case, it wanted to avoid all other craft.

8

Plan of Action

THE ENGINE purred like a stroked cat. We were making five or six knots now, instead of three or four, and the exhaust was only one half as noisy as it had been. And we were heading away from Luzon for the last time. Thunderheads were coming up in the east and dirty weather was gathering strength to spring on us.

I took the first watch. We had three boat compasses and, checking them, found they had little, if any, deviation. One of them was particularly good, so we rigged a screened light for it, powered by the Diesel starting battery. By the time Taylor came back to take his trick at the tiller it had grown rougher. I showed him the few stars that were visible, told him their names and how they would move during his watch, and explained how he could pick out any convenient star and steer by it. If the star he picked was high in the sky he'd have to correct his compass every fifteen minutes or so. If the star was low he could allow a half-hour. We kept the little screened light in the compass turned off except during checking.

We were tossing pretty badly, and at four o'clock a

Plan of Action

green one came overside which woke us up, cursing. There was six inches of water in the boat, and the men went to work bailing. But the green ones kept coming over and it was all the men could do to keep even with them.

My next idea was to go back to help Taylor with the tiller. But he was doing all right. It was the weather that was doing all wrong. The waves kicked up not big rollers but nasty, short, choppy waves, from six to eight feet high. With only a short interval between them, they were more dangerous to a boat our size than big ocean rollers would have been. I tried to help by giving Taylor advice on easing the tiller so the bow would fall off before each oncoming wave.

The men weren't worried, only grumpy about being wet and having to slog away at the endless task of trying to empty the ocean back into the ocean. They were cold from the spray and green water and driving rain but they had discovered the trick of putting their bare feet in the bilges where the sea water was warmer than the rain.

Dawn came up cold and dismal. We could see nothing but gray water and in the far distance the low streak of black on the horizon which was Masbate.

We wanted coffee now and we wanted it bad. Back at a previous stop we had made a stove out of a five-gallon oil tin and mounted it on a bed of sand in a flat box. We had also purchased a quantity of raw brown sugar at our last stop. The firewood was sopping wet, so we drained out a half cupful of Diesel oil from the tanks and poured it over the sticks. We had cut the top out of the can, bent its front back like a flap, and hung a water bucket down inside it. The general effect was shaky, but we managed to prop it up so that nothing tragic happened. When the water boiled we poured coffee into it and threw in an eggshell. Newquist had been keeping up a running fire of talk about how his mother made the world's best coffee on the farm back in Kansas. The eggshell was his touch.

Sweetening the brew was a problem. The sea water had got into the brown sugar and hardened it into a lump of rocklike consistency. We borrowed a file from the engineer and jabbed away at it until we broke it up. The fragrant, hot fluid went down inside of us, socking against the insides of our stomachs with a warm, heartening glow, and we felt better. Breakfast was rice thinned out with canned milk and topped off with raw sugar and sliced bananas, and it was our standard breakfast from then on.

At eight o'clock the clouds broke up and a tropical sun looked through. By ten o'clock we were panting, and our tongues were as dry as the beef the natives had jerked for us.

The water quieted to a dead calm, and we chugged along steadily due south. All day long we passed along the coastline of Masbate, watching it suspiciously. It was one of the first islands the Japs had taken over, and we knew they were in there as thick as maggots on a carcass. To the west were the high peaks of Sibuyan Island, and we kept closer to them because they were less dangerous.

Our hunch about the scarcity of ships in this area paid off. We didn't sight a single ship or boat throughout that long, hot day.

We figured that, since this had proved to be a spot in which we were not likely to run into enemy ships, our

Plan of Action

best bet was to keep going even though it meant traveling in revealing daylight.

We were sure there would be strong currents among the numerous channels and islands, but we didn't know in which direction these currents would run. In the morning we found out. They were running against us.

We stood up and gave the horizon the gimlet eye. Dead ahead was Malapascua Island, and Steele said in his slow drawl, "I wouldn't want to upset you, Captain, but that looks a hell of a lot like the two masts of a destroyer up against that island." The ship appeared to be anchored hull down, and I yelled up to the bow, where Haley and Clarke were sitting on their lookout watch, to tell them to get their heads down. Steele and I slipped down into the engine compartment, where we steered and watched with our eyes just over the edge of the gunwale.

Our crew of sleeping beauties popped their heads up, but when Steele and I told them there was a destroyer ahead they quit rubbernecking. Our idea was that with no heads sticking up, the boat, seen from dead ahead, would be indistinguishable from a log or a native banca. We went on cautiously, waiting for the deckhouse and silhouette of the destroyer to appear, which they gradually did. It was high time for us to take refuge somewhere. The crew were holed up in the bow of the boat, cleaning their rifles and pistols, just as if the destroyer we had seen was a boat no bigger than ours and an even match. They were outwardly nonchalant, but I could feel their tenseness.

About eight o'clock we got in the shelter of a little island. Our next problem was whether to keep on to Leyte or try for Cebu. It was twenty miles to Leyte across open water, and the coast of Cebu looked a better bet. So we made a dash for it. In close to the beach there were landing beaches and a number of beautiful homes. On the beach we could see natives going from one house to another. We were only a hundred yards out and our white faces must have been plainly visible, but the natives didn't come down to visit us. They just went about their business.

I asked Taylor, "Guns, what do you make of it?"

And he said, "I don't like it."

I agreed with him. "Let's get the hell out of here," I said, and we got away from there fast.

Later on we found out from a Filipino family in Palompon who helped us that the cold shoulder these natives gave us had saved our lives. Jap soldiers were occupying those beautiful homes, but, as usual, in the absence of some definite military reason to rise and shine, they were late sleepers. On shore, outnumbered and fighting in a land fight, we would have been easy pickings for them. The Palompon family had lived on Cebu and knew the danger we had barely avoided. They had had a summer home on that very shore but had to run for it because their political leanings were suspected when the Japs came.

Just as we made up our minds we didn't want any part of Cebu, Head dropped our chart overboard. In our overwrought state we wanted to kill him right then and there. He was one of those guys who endear themselves to you one minute and the next you want to cut their throat. We put Watkins overside to fish the chart up from the coral since we couldn't get the boat in close enough to pick it up. Having made up our minds the place was bad medicine,

Plan of Action

we wanted to get clear of it in a hurry, but without our chart we couldn't go anywhere.

We decided to cut across to Leyte after all. We passed through a narrow channel and as we stuck our nose around the corner of Bulalaqui we nearly bumped into a Jap ship. It was a tanker heading almost directly for us, about six thousand yards away. They had probably seen us, and if we turned around and headed for Cebu it would look suspicious. Besides, Cebu, we felt instinctively, was bad news. I looked at that tanker and noted that the opening between its masts formed a very small angle, which meant that it would be a matter of only a few moments before we crossed its path and put it behind us on our port quarter. It shaped up into the kind of problem a submarine commander faces every time he angles a torpedo at a moving target. The tanker was going about four hundred yards a minute; it would take her about fifteen minutes to get to the spot where we would cross over in front of her. We were making about two hundred yards a minute, so at our closest point of contact we would be about three thousand yards apart. At that distance our only hope was to keep everybody out of sight and, since we were not making any hostile moves, she might assume we were a Jap patrol boat. I put Taylor, who had black hair like a Jap, on the tiller, told him to keep his face turned away, and covered the rest of the boys up with the tarp.

I don't know why it worked out, but it did. Apparently they never gave us a serious thought. When she was out of sight we came to life and had breakfast. Newquist said, "Boy, it sure would have been tough if old Taylor's head had turned gray from the strain back there when we were picking ourselves out of that Jap's teeth."

By this time we had worked up a definite dislike for our surroundings and wanted to put as much room as soon as possible between ourselves and Cebu. Keeping eastward we headed into Tobangas Bay, getting there about eleven o'clock in the morning, much later than we had hoped. Feeling our way through a winding channel we tied our boat up to a little stone jetty.

There, waiting for us, was a tall Filipino and standing beside him was a Chinese merchant. We asked them if there was any place where we could buy lubricating oil, Diesel oil, Manila sail line, and canned food.

The Filipino introduced himself and said, "My father is waiting for you and he will see that you get everything you need."

I told Cucinello to keep enough men in the boat to clean her up and stand watch and take the rest of them and go up to the town to see what he could buy. Five of us, including Taylor and myself, stayed behind. Crowds of natives milled around, talking in soft voices. Presently Taylor and I left Haley and Watkins in the boat and went uptown, too. On the dock we were met by Head coming back. He told us that a wealthy, elderly Filipino wanted to see us and that the rest of our boys were up at his house. Everything seemed just too, too clubby.

I questioned him sharply about the crew.

He just grinned and said, "Oh, they're all right. They're doing fine."

We walked a few blocks up a cobblestoned street to a big showplace of a mansion and started up a long flight of steps. Seeing that ornate house we were suddenly conscious of the fact that we were dirty and unshaven, and I said to Head, "We aren't dressed to go into a dump like this."

As we stood there with half a mind to go back we looked up at the top of the stairs and saw a white-haired man with arms outstretched in welcome. "Come right up," he said. "I am so glad to see you."

I said something about us looking like bums, but he pooh-poohed that kind of talk. "The clothes are not important," he said. "Here you are welcome. I have all your boys, the poor young ones." He sounded like something out of a book.

I stepped into a large living room. Head hadn't missed it very far. The "poor young ones" were making out very nicely indeed. They were perched on overstuffed ottomans and draped on easy chairs, drinking cold lemonade served to them by a bevy of beautiful young girls, all of whom looked like Dorothy Lamour.

"What would your poor young ones like to eat?" asked our host, and I picked the name of a food out of the air.

"They like bread," I told him. "They haven't had any for a long time."

He clapped his hands together like a character out of the *Arabian Nights* calling up a couple of jinn and said to two or three of the Lamour numbers, "We must bake bread quickly." I pinched myself mentally. But it was all true. He seated me in state and I was drinking lemonade and eating little frosted cakes too.

Then, remembering our self-consciousness about feeling grubby, he said, "You give clothes to laundry girls. They wash right away." I explained that we couldn't do that because our clothes were all on our backs and we would feel pretty odd running around naked. He took care of that. "My son will take your men a little way down the street to a public bathhouse, and you and your chief assistants can use my own bathroom." For a bathtub in an establishment straight out of a Hollywood movie or a dream book his bathtub was a disappointment. It was a portable iron, coffin-like arrangement, and our experience with it didn't do us much good. The place was like a Turkish bath. We went in dirty and came out clean, but we had to put our dirty clothes back on and emerged, dripping sweat.

The men made out much better than we did, since they were able to wash their clothes and dry them in the afternoon sun.

After a while I rounded up Head and Meeker—Meeker to buy provisions and Head to do the talking. Haley came along to purchase more rigging, and we all went down to the Chinese store. We bought almost their entire stock of coffee, eggs, and sardines, and paid for it out of the common pool of money. The next thing we thought of was clothing. Everywhere we had been, our khaki had shouted out loud to any onlooker that we were American soldiers while we were still a long way off. We had bought straw hats at a previous stop but had lost most of them in the rough weather. After this we made chin straps with our shoestrings to hold them on. Head cut the gold leaf from my collar with his medical scissors to keep me from being singled out to be shot or for an extra-special slapping around or torture if we were captured, but the sun had left the imprint of the insignia behind it, and there was a telltale, sharply defined unbleached area whose implications completely nullified Head's operation.

There was a great confab among the men as to the proper color for their new clothing. The Chinese haberdashery offered a wide assortment of red, orange, and dungaree blue. The red and orange we thought too visible and the blue too similar to a soldier or sailor's work costume, so we dug down further and finally settled on a gray-green prison-suit combination. After the first rain we wore them in, these clothes shrank small enough to fit a teddy bear.

When we finished our purchases, the Chinese invited us to a Chinese restaurant just around the corner. We climbed to the restaurant's second floor and were greeted by a luncheon layout of cold sliced meats, sandwiches, and cheeses. Liquor was conspicuously on tap. There were whisky and beer for the boys, and the Chinese insisted on my having a tumbler of brandy. There was a plentiful supply of Chinese girls on hand, together with a sprinkling of *mestizas* (girls with half-Filipino and half-Chinese blood), and things had all the makings of an all-out party. The girls told the boys that if they would hang around that evening they would throw a dance for them. I was still a long way away from having a yen to celebrate. Moreover, the setup was too alluring and pat. I whispered to Richardson, "I'm going to excuse myself. You get the boys out of here. It may be perfectly all right, but we don't want to be caught off guard doing research into the manners and morals of *mestizas* if the Japs walk in on us."

I left with Taylor, and Richardson passed the word around. It came as a shock to the boys, but they followed us out, grumbling only a little. Looking back on it, it seems queer that there wasn't more bellyaching from them about being deprived of what in peacetime would have been a big night on the town. But at the time it didn't seem strange.

Up on the bridge before we got into the war I had overheard conversations from the crew, and a lot of them were about some cutie who was fun on a party or some dame with a generous nature. But not once in all of the five months after December 7 did I hear a crack made on the *Quail* that would indicate that sex was uppermost in anybody's mind. My gang weren't Milquetoasts, God knows. They just weren't interested in sleeping with anybody else when they were already sleeping with death.

If any psychologist wants to find out which one of the two instincts, sex or fear, is the strongest, I can tell them. Fear wins in a walk. Our minds were full of killing or being killed, and frolicking femmes were something that could wait until we had achieved security. But one thing I know: the Japs didn't think we were panty-waists.

At the bathing pools the natives showed us the men didn't blink an eye at seeing naked native women with water glistening on smooth flanks and round bellies. But having the women see them stripped embarrassed them. It had nothing to do with the war chasing sex out of their minds. They would have felt that way, war or no war. They were simple souls to whom group exposure seemed perverted and contrary to the decent privacy which they felt should veil mixed nakedness.

On the *Quail* we didn't envy the men on Bataan or Corregidor who managed to get dates with the nurses. We couldn't understand people thinking in terms of dates when

Plan of Action

the old man with the scythe was rustling his robes over our heads.

Actually I think those Chinese merchants were trying to be friendly, but with liquor flowing copiously and the willing and co-operative female talent it seemed much safer for people in our precarious position to be up at the elderly planter's house minding our P's and Q's like good little boys. Our host's wife began to supervise some of her daughters and granddaughters in the running back and forth, the scurrying and excitement, of getting together a colossal meal for us. We begged them not to take any extra trouble, but one of the sons had gone out and shot some wild pigs and they were dead set on having a barbecue for us.

The mamma of the family was enormous. Filipino women do not usually grow fat, but she was short, broad, and huge.

I said to our host, "It's mighty good of you to take stranded people into your home like this," and the old gentleman said with implicit faith, "If we were shipwrecked on the California coast your people would look out for us and take care of us."

It made us stop for a minute and wonder if our own people back home would be so quick to take in disheveled, tramplike strangers if they came knocking at their doors. We mentioned these doubts, but the old man said, "You are being too modest. The American people have big hearts."

We sat down around a table huge enough to seat all of us and ten or twelve of the family besides. Some of the food was strange but all of it was good. The table was heaped with flowers, and the air was spicy with their fragrance. There were white tablecloths, shining silver, delicate china plates. The daughters of the household served the food and made our boys feel like princes. When it was over, the old planter, his older sons, Taylor, and I went into his private study. We asked him how the war was affecting him.

"For me," he said, "I've had forty years of the good life."

One of his sons spoke up, "When the Americans came and took the islands, Papa cried. When the Japs took the islands he cried again, but in between times it was all happiness for us."

The old man was curious about how I had selected my crew for the escape attempt and asked me if they had been leaders on shipboard. "We have some of the highest and lowest ratings with us," I told him. "I didn't select them. They selected me."

It was true. If I had picked the men to go along I probably wouldn't have selected the ones fate handed me. But you get to know people's insides as well as their outsides living as we lived, practically in each other's pockets. Insight into what makes a man's wheels go round comes easy when you're cooped up together on a boat the size of an apartment hallway, and I wouldn't have traded one of them for anybody else I knew.

Taken as a group they were like any other handful of young men dumped down together by luck. They were simple, lusty, and natural. They took both their high moments and low depths big, going all-out for each one. They

Plan of Action

kidded and needled each other. They were trigger-tempered and edgy when confinement in close quarters and strain got them down, yet you could see them growing up and maturing hourly. In their serious moments their habits of thought were those of young men made old before they ought to be by having seen men die violently; by experience with physical exhaustion, and by the knowledge of defeat, no less bitter because they believed with passionate conviction it was only a temporary setback.

You could have tossed them into any shirt-sleeved, polo-jerseyed, bleacher-seat crowd taking in a big-league holiday double-header, and they would have fitted in.

Listening to them and watching them during the long hours, when the Diesel throbbed endlessly and the water unrolled under us, I got a picture of them as individuals, with different backgrounds.

Nick Cucinello had joined the Navy on the first birthday that made him old enough. His father had kept the family going by toiling as a day laborer, and Nick had helped out by juggling huge blocks of ice in a wholesale ice company. He looked like a cross between Laurence Olivier and Francis Lederer, and he was blessed with a larger supply of sheer courage than any man I've ever known, which is saying plenty since none of the seventeen could be accused of gutlessness.

Some days before the fall of Bataan, he had been sent on detached duty to serve as a watchman on a merchant ship filled with bombs and high explosive tied up on the Bataan shore. The Nips threw everything at that ship except their ceremonial hara-kiri knives. The remnants of the regular crew climbed into a ship's boat and departed from the scene, and Cucinello found himself alone on her decks. He never thought of going with them. The Nip aim got better, and an incendiary bomb set the ship on fire. Cucinello managed to put the blaze out singlehanded, but the fire was the least of his worries. There he was, all alone, a Boy on the Burning Deck Whence All But Him Had Fled, if there ever was one, and he felt his responsibility keenly. There was no one around to give him orders; the ship with its deadly cargo was strictly his baby. And it weighed on his mind.

Finally, it was obvious that Bataan's end was only a matter of hours, even minutes. The Japs were fighting down at the water's edge. Cucinello did what he thought he should do. He set a demolition charge to make sure the ship didn't fall into their hands and rowed away in a dinghy.

The demolition charge did its stuff, and when the ship exploded the concussion picked up Cucinello and his tiny craft and lifting them bodily into the air crashed them onto the Bataan rocks. Lying there stunned, he saw the last boat passing on its way back to Corregidor with a load of escaping men. He hailed them and they took him off.

Now, after a day when the water lay warm in the breakers of our open boat, in his sleep he dreamed of chunks of ice tinkling against the sides of tall glasses and pitchers, cool and dripping. It must have been that his early ice-handling days gave him these visions. He hadn't been home for eight years, but the meals his mother had dished up in Bloomfield, New Jersey, were more real to him now than they had been when set smoking before him.

"There's a trick to handling those two-hundred-pound

Plan of Action

blocks of ice," he told the others. "You do it just right and it's easy." He had a well-developed sense of drama and was acutely aware of the excitement of our days. "I could write a book," he said. "I could write a whole book about just one day back on Bataan."

He was an embryo philosopher, too. "These things change a guy," he said. "They make you look at things kind of different, like you didn't look at 'em before."

Swisher was small-boned and fair, with a thinning crop of tow-colored hair. He had followed the harvests in the Middle West and worked for a farm-machinery manufacturing company. He had made an improvement on the machine and had been given a hundred shares of stock as payment. "Sometimes that stock pays me a few bucks," he said, "and sometimes I have to send the company a few bucks to help out." He had been Assistant Scout Master of Troop 16, Council Bluffs, Iowa, and an Eagle Scout lacking but one badge of having all the scout badges there were.

Stringer was an erect and quiet Texan and, like all Texans, a fanatical partisan for the Lone Star State. You could get an argument out of him any time by merely dropping a derogatory remark about the home of the Longhorn, Davy Crockett, and the Alamo. The boys found it out and bore down hard, but Stringer never failed to come up verbally swinging and loyal. He had been a farmer, "not a rancher," he was careful to explain. When his thoughts turned to food he thought of antelope meat. "I had a pal at Arizona State Teachers I used to go hunting with," he told us. "They took me in and treated me practically like a member of the family. I don't know why."

Then he'd get a dreamy, faraway look in his eyes and murmur, "Antelope meat is a lot sweeter than deer meat."

Newquist was an Iowa farm product, a big hulk of a boy, open-faced and blond, who loved to eat and drink everything anybody put before him. He was easygoing and wore a slow grin, even when, back at Pearl Harbor, my children met him and took him in hand to improve his English, telling him he shouldn't say, "ain't."

Rankin's father was in the rug-cleaning business at Long Beach, California. Like Head, Rankin had left home pretty much in the doghouse, with his father feeling he would never amount to anything. It was their lifetime ambition to prove to their respective dads that they were dead wrong. As far as I am concerned they can stop worrying about that. If their fathers aren't satisfied, they are hard to please.

Head was from Kentucky. He had flecks of gray at his temples and his head was set deep between his shoulders, giving him a slightly stooped appearance. He didn't really stoop; he just looked that way.

Mentioning half a dozen of them ought to give a rough cross section of what breed of men they were. They were an average slice of America.

We could hear a little hum of conversation out on the veranda, and the old man took my arm, saying, "Let's see what your boys are doing." Peering around a corner we saw them seated on a long row of chairs along one side of the porch. Facing them was an equally long row of girls. Each row was leaning forward engaged in earnest conversation with the one opposite.

He went back to the study, brought out large wall maps,

Plan of Action

and we engaged in a lively discussion of the best route for us to take and how we could best avoid the Jap picket boats and get clear of this eastward fringe of the islands. Each son and son-in-law had a pet theory.

The father listened to what everyone had to say and then said his piece. "Now listen to me. Today and tomorrow the Japs will be busy interning your soldiers in the various concentration points throughout the islands. The next day they will have their victory celebration. For one more day they will be no good because of drink and girls. That gives you three, maybe four, days in which you may be safe. After that, the Japs will be looking for you and all like you. You must be clear of the islands by the fourth day. One of my sons says to go through San Bernardino Strait and one says the narrow strait between Samar and Leyte. I will tell you what to do. You go south as far as you can, then quick you must go through the Surigao Strait at night, then south and south and south until no more you see the Philippines."

I had a rough plan like that in my head already, but without his warning I might have made more stops on Leyte. He particularly warned me not to stop on Leyte, and whereas I had been planning to run only at night he warned me to keep going day and night.

The talk had drawn us well into the evening. It was approaching high water in the channel again and time for us to leave. We made our farewells. As each man left, the old man embraced him and said, "You'll get away, never fear." Tears were streaming down his face.

We went stumbling down to the boat along the cobblestoned road in the growing darkness, led by three of his sons. The boat was not quite afloat and one of the sons got in to act as pilot. The other two went along the shore to the outer harbor to bring him back in a small boat when he had finished helping us. The water grew higher, and we floated out, poling her through winding channels. We grounded in several places and each time had to wait a few minutes for the water to rise and lift us off. Toward the outer end of the channel our pilot told us we were approaching a place where we would either make it or fail and have to turn back. We had come in during the daytime high, and the night high tide was two or three feet lower. We neared the shallowest spot of all when the tide was just about at its peak. As we hit this spot we grounded solidly. "You must pole now if you are going to get over," the pilot said. So pole we did. We poled and tugged until it seemed almost as if we lifted the boat up by main strength and shoved it over that mudbank. As we slipped over the outer edge, our pilot said, "You just made it. The water has turned and is going down."

The sons went back to the beach and we set a course close to the southern edge of the mouth of the bay. Clearing the point, we heard the high-pitched sound of an airplane or speedboat motor. Squatting down and looking through the night glasses, we made it out to be quite a good-sized power boat heading into the bay we had just left. Whether it was a Jap patrol boat or not we never found out. The important thing was it didn't come after us or catch up with us.

The water was smooth, the moon was high, the breeze velvet against our faces. The men sat around and talked, calf-eyed about the girls they had left back on that veranda.

In spite of our narrow squeak with the patrol boat, the war seemed a long way off. Chugging along through the night southward we felt a sense of security and peace we hadn't felt for five long months.

The old gentleman had managed to impress upon us his belief that everything was going to be all right. It was as though he had put a benediction upon us. He had been old and wise and experienced and he had spoken with an air of authority, almost as if, being so old, he could look into the future as well as the past.

9

Dodging the Red-balls

THE DAWN broke in the east on a misty, drizzling rain. We were coming to the Camotes Islands ahead. Looking over toward the city of Cebu very carefully, we could see the topmasts of many ships going in and out, but they were too far away to see us and we merely changed our course slightly to the southeast to pass closer to Leyte, where the water was freer from traffic. We were now getting down close to an area where none of us had ever been before and it was difficult to identify the various little islands and jutting rocks. We had no pelorus with which to spot a fix, but Binkley and I learned a number of tricks, such as using two points of land, opening or closing on each other, as a bearing which we could check roughly by holding our small boat compass in our hands and sighting along its top. We worked it out by elimination. We'd get two objects in sight, take their bearing with our compass, and then consulting our chart we'd eliminate all the places we couldn't be, finally boiling it down to the one of two places where we must be.

We went on through the Camotes Sea without any difficulty. The sun was not too hot and it was very pleasant. Some of the tightened springs coiled inside of us began to unwind. We had our usual two meals, with coffee at frequent intervals between them.

Disconnected scenes and pictures had a way of leaping out of the back of my mind when I had nothing else to do but lean on the tiller and watch the waves roll wetly toward us out of the place where they were born, on the other side of the horizon.

One picture I kept seeing for no reason at all was the day I had gone over to Mariveles to take one of my men to do some special radio work in the *Canopus'* radio shop. On the way back we passed through a small Filipino village near the beach. Two small native boys about seven or eight years old were playing there, using lumps of dirt for toys. A flight of Jap bombers sailed over, moving flyspecks dirtying a spotless robin's-egg-blue sky. The two children looked up, saw that the line of Jap flight would carry them off to one side of their village, and went on playing.

That particular flight dropped its eggs on the Baguio hospital—it was the first time they had bombed it—and a second flight came over right above us. The kids looked up again, unhurried and casual but wise in intensive experience with such things. We could see them gauging the angle and deciding that this time the Japs were going to mail them a special-delivery package. They moved calm and unperturbed over to a low spot behind an outcropping of rocks and lay down still clutching their dirt playthings.

By this time I was back in the boat that had brought me to Bataan. I heard the familiar freight-train rattle of bombs dropping and for a moment nothing happened. Then there was a flaring Bunsen-burner jet of reddish-orange flame, speckled with black spots of bomb fragments and mushrooming earth. When each bomb landed, the flame from it licked over and joined the flame of the others, giving the effect of a long, horizontal flame.

When it was all over and the bomb craters were still smoking, the two kids picked themselves up and waded out into the shallow water near the beach with baskets to collect the fish killed by the concussion of one of the bombs that had missed a Q boat tied up there. They were practically naked and just babies, but they were seasoned veterans for all that, and a bombing more or less meant nothing to them, except as in this case when it brought them their dinner.

We were far away from bombs now. If a plane with the rising sun on its wings found us we would be in for a machine-gun strafing or, if not that, a report radioed back to a Jap destroyer. Bombs would have been easier. Our boat moved fast enough not to be there by the time one could plummet down at us.

Rounding the southwest end of Leyte about dusk, we stopped to feed the engine, too. It was quite an operation. We had to siphon the oil out of the drum into a can and empty the can into the engine tanks. While that was going on, Haley and the rest of the crew straightened up the boat, secured the gear for the sea, and put safety lines around the oil drums so they wouldn't roll around if the waves took us for a ride. We prepared the floor boards for bailing and got the bailing cans out. Sure enough, when we hit the Surigao Strait the water chopped up. Mean, black-looking clouds curtained the sky and a cold drizzle set in. The men huddled together in the bow and tried to sleep.

Instead of going through the main part of the strait, where we might have run into Jap ships, I decided to take the boat through the channel south of Dinagat Island. On the schoolbook maps it shows as a wide-open place. Actually it was chock-a-block with small swampy islands which only show up when you get on top of them. We expected a strong current in the Surigao Strait but we had to cross it to get to the narrow southern passage. With good visibility this would have been no great trick but in soupy weather we couldn't see anything ahead and had to estimate the strength and direction of the current in order to stand a chance of arriving at the proper gap between the small islands we were heading for. Sure enough, after passing open water, when we sighted land it was close aboard. It seemed as if there were three possible entrances to the channel, although we knew there was only one. For all we knew, the current had been much stronger than we thought and we were running into one of the small creeks or rivers of the island itself.

Again we used our process of elimination. We ran up and down the coast, sighting through these various channels, squinting along the top of our compass until we found the only one whose axis had a bearing like the one on the chart. Running down the channel we reached the place we were supposed to turn, when the shore seemed to close in on us from all sides. A thousand yards ahead of us was a large mudbank where we could easily get stuck high and dry until daylight came, and in this case waiting for daylight might well mean waiting for duration since we were near the city of Surigao, where the Japs were interning our troops from Mindanao.

Just when it looked worst, almost as if by magic the left bank opened up and we could see the channel to the north of us. Binkley and Steele weren't sure even then, but something told me that in two more jogs we'd be all right, and we were. We jogged left, went a few hundred yards more, jogged right, then all at once through an ever-widening broad channel we saw the open water of the Pacific.

It was the first time we had been in it since we'd come out from Honolulu.

That night it treated us gently, rolling us with a swinging lullaby motion. When dawn broke clear and bright we saw several coves on the shore line and ducked into one. Working our way through reefs and coral heads we got ourselves into an inner cove landlocked and obscured from view in all directions. It had no name on our chart, but they could have called it Coral Gables or Catalina and it would have been O.K. with us. It was ringed with white sand and palm trees. The water cupped in it was crystal clear and peopled with queer-looking fish swimming sassy around the boat. It was hard to be old man gloom in such surroundings but it seemed to me important that at least one of us keep squared away on the idea that we weren't on any picnic. And we had two potential enemies to cope with now instead of one, for the open sea could be terrifying as well as friendly, depending on its mood. We still had about thirteen hundred more miles to go. Our boat was low in the water, wide and flat-beamed, and not built like a lifeboat by any manner of means.

No sooner had we reached the beach than natives appeared, coming down out of the hills, bearing fruit. We asked them if there was any water near by, and they showed us. A Philippine aqueduct made of bamboo trees split in half with the webs cut out so that they formed open pipes overlapping one another stretched over forked sticks running up the mountainside. At the bottom, it dumped its burden over a big boulder and formed a pool. We stood under it and had another bath. When I finished I went back to the camp and caught up on my sleep. I woke up to the sound of excited voices.

"Maybe these people are used to it, but it kind of makes me feel funny."

I rolled over and asked what it was all about.

"We were minding our own business," the men said, "just taking a bath when, bam!—the place was full of women taking baths, too."

After dinner we tried out the sail. Haley looked at it darkly and said it was a hell of a sail. We all knew it was a hell of a sail but we tried to comfort him by describing its good points, which were hard to find. The canvas it was made of, having been originally the fo'c'sle awning on our ship, was too heavy for a small boat, and Haley was afraid that in any kind of wind it might turn us over.

While we were on the subject of motive power, we checked our figures on fuel consumption. Binkley provided the figures for the miles covered so far, and the engineers gave us the amount of oil used to date. We were getting about four miles a gallon. At that rate we would barely get to Australia by the skin of our teeth and only then if we didn't run into bad weather, which was almost inevitable.

The men wanted to know what kind of weather we

would run into in the Dutch East Indies, and the question, like many of their questions, threw me for a loss. I'd never been there, and we had failed to find the necessary books on the *Ranger* that day we left which would have given me the answer. I tried to conjure up the tag ends of the memories of everything I'd ever read on the subject. All I could remember was a horrible tale about a super-typhoon which had started in Java and had lasted for weeks and months. That was just fiction and didn't mean anything. Still, I couldn't remember anything consoling about the weather there. All my recollections seemed to be full of torrential rains and sudden devastating gusts of wind. I remembered also hearing over the radio that a large number of Jap troops had been drowned by a cloudburst in New Guinea. When it came to a showdown, I told myself I'd figure things out against my background of knowledge of trade winds and ocean currents. I got out the chart and traced the paths of the north trades, the south trades, the winds of the roaring forties west of Australia, and the southwest monsoon which came up from India. It looked to me as if all the winds in that half of the hemisphere met somewhere in the Dutch East Indies and staged a battle royal to see which one would be head man.

In the late afternoon we took down the mast and headed back into the Pacific. Night came on, bringing with it the same thunderheads and drizzling rain we hoped we had said good-by to that morning. The visibility was low, and we didn't dare go too close to shore for fear of hitting a reef. I covered myself up with a poncho and stretched out on a corner of the thwart, folded up like a jackknife. Bent over that way, I could brace myself, even when I was sleeping, against the rolling and pitching. But my instinctive muscular reactions didn't help when a wave dumped itself into my lap about four o'clock in the morning. I woke up going through swimming motions. The feeling you get when you wake up like that isn't a good one. Your first fear is that you are going to drown; your next is that you are not going to. You are miserable and cold. Then you get a little more awake and realize that the boat hasn't sunk yet but that once more you are in a hell of a fix.

We were headed directly up into the wind. I took the tiller from Taylor and swung her hard over with full speed on the engine. As soon as we got the sea on our quarter and stern, the boat rode like a piece of floating soap in a bathtub. Now our only difficulty was that the wind was driving us back toward the beach and the rocks, but by keeping the wind and the sea far around on our port quarter, we reduced our drift beachward. Before those rocks got too dangerous it would be morning and we could find another cove. When daylight came we were still quite a way off the land and we picked out a good-sized bay which was a part of Lianga Bay, just north of Port Lamon.

It looked good to us from the sea, but as we approached it we discovered a pretty rough surf ahead of us. As we got closer I saw a good-sized break in the surf and went through it carefully into deep water. Once inside and behind the protection of the point things were as quiet and serene as they had been turbulent before. There was a small dock and beyond that were some native houses. On the dock were a couple of stacks of lumber. There were thousands of Japs on the island of Mindanao and if we found them we were going to be definitely trapped. It was too rough for us at sea and we couldn't turn around and go back out again even if we bumped into a detachment of Jap soldiers.

We cruised a few tentative circles before we entered the inner port but, not having seen any tents, barracks, or signs of troop activities, we decided to take a chance. We didn't have much choice.

When we stepped on the dock a little, runty, half-pint Filipino came out to meet us. He said he was sorry that no one had come out to show us the channel, but that they'd thought we were a Jap patrol boat. He wigwagged to the natives back among the trees, who came pouring down the hillside and explained to us that they had all worked in a sawmill at Port Lamon but a typhoon had destroyed the mill. The mill workers, up till that time, had subsisted on food shipped in from Manila. Now they had taken up farming in order to exist. He apologized for not having any food to give us.

"My people are city people," he said. "They do not know much farming."

"Don't worry about food," we told him. "We've got a lot." And asked him if he and his group would like to eat with us.

He refused, saying, "In a short time we will have plenty to eat and you will need yours."

The natives came down from the hills by ones and twos and tried to give us some pitiful-looking specimens of wild papaya and wrinkled, shriveled *camotes*, which we refused even at the risk of hurting their feelings. If they wouldn't take food from us, at least we could see to it they kept what they had.

Dodging the Red-balls

Those stacks of lumber gave us a bright idea. It would be swell if we had sideboards on our boat so the green water wouldn't roll over us so easily, and we asked the natives if they could spare a few planks.

"You are welcome," they told us. "We have all we want."

Then we got another brain storm. Why not deck over the boat? The Navy had never decked over this type of boat, but we felt under the circumstances the Navy wouldn't mind.

Steele asked them if they had any Diesel oil, and to our surprise they answered that they had a couple of drums salvaged from Port Lamon.

"It is up in the hills," they said, "but we are glad to roll them down for you."

It would take all that day and part of the next morning to deck over the boat, so we told them the next morning would be all right. We all turned to and became boat-builders.

Decking over a boat sounds simple, but it is an intricate and tricky proposition. It has to be braced from underneath just right. There must be overlaps and combings made for the edges to keep the boards from being pushed loose by the sea hammering at them.

While the self-appointed master carpenters were chiseling and sawing, I told Steele that it was about time we got to work on a sextant and we hashed over a possible substitute. In the end our best bet seemed to be to make the simplest frame we could use for sighting angles. There would be two arms with a place for the eye near the pivot. One arm would point at the horizon and the other at the sun. As we visualized it, the thing would look very much like a pair of dividers. Then, after obtaining the right angle, we would tighten the set screw which held the device together where the two arms joined, and the next step would be to take the whole device and lay it down on a large piece of graduated paper. On this paper we had inscribed the angles with a pencil.

Steele took two old pieces of a parallel ruler, split them, and bored a hole in them for his set screw. After trying it out I decided that under good conditions I could read it to within half a degree. If the boat were rolling or pitching I might finish up as much as one degree off, which would probably mean an error of from thirty to sixty miles in finding out our position at sea. In the ordinary course of events dead reckoning would be more accurate than our home-grown stunt, but if we ran into a period of stormy weather and were driven off our course, it would be accurate enough to help us locate ourselves after the storm and keep us from missing the large islands.

By the time darkness fell, we had all the supporting timbers and boards cut but hadn't got down to putting them together, and they were still littering up the boat when we knocked off and called it a day.

The village head man invited Taylor and myself up to his house to share his nonexistent fare. There was almost no food but great pomp. Taylor and myself sat with him and his wife. He spoke of his terror of the Japs coming to the village. He skipped the horrible things the Japs had done to his people. That was all right with me. I didn't need another load of atrocity stories to make me hate the Japs any better. I hated plenty good the way it was.

Dodging the Red-balls

Taylor and I slept under the edge of a lumber pile at the dock end. The two men on watch sat on top of it. Our eyes and ears were getting pretty sharp. Even in our sleep we seemed to be listening, and ruled out no sounds as casual and trivial until we had found out where they came from and who was making them.

Shortly after we dropped off to sleep both Taylor and I sat up with a start and looked to seaward. Above us the two lookouts were cupping their hands to their ears. Later when we compared notes we found out that all of the men who were sleeping in the house ashore had pricked up their ears at the same moment. What we had heard was a faint, faraway drone, more like a drawn-out sigh than a noise. I asked Taylor what he made of it. He said he didn't know.

"It must be the wind bringing the sound of the surf breaking out there on the reef in to us," he said.

Gradually it got louder and more unmistakable, and we didn't have to ask each other what it was. It was the familiar song of a Jap patrol boat.

The feeling of being in a trap came back to us, doubled and redoubled.

I said to Head, "Go call the boys and tell them to get into the boat and break out the guns."

He had only taken about ten steps when he bumped into the whole kit and caboodle of them rushing in our direction. Telling our lookouts to keep down behind the lumber piles, Cucinello, Taylor, Meeker, Head, and I went into a committee on getting ourselves out of there and saving eighteen skins.

But most of all we wanted to save the boat. The boat meant freedom, and we were pretty attached to that commodity by this time. We could always take to the hills and possibly elude pursuit for months while we were being man-hunted and tracked down, but we didn't find the idea of being dogged by the Japs in the wooded rising land very appealing. Perhaps we were a little spoiled by our survival thus far, but if there was any chasing to be done, we wanted to be the ones doing it and not have the Japs always barking at our heels.

The skin-saving committee decided that we'd stay where we were and move the boat along the shore a little way to a place where it would be out of the way of stray bullets, if the night wound up in a shooting war.

The menacing chug-chug outside came to us in greatly increased volume. We realized that probably there were a whole string of boats out there.

"I don't care if they've got the papa and mamma patrol boat and all of the little patrol boats out there; they can only come at us one at a time, and if we throw enough stuff at 'em they might stall and send for destroyer help," Steele said. "Then at high tide we can slip along the shore and skin out through the whole works."

We might not have an advantage in numbers but we had one other advantage—our boat only drew four feet of water and the usual Jap patrol boat drew eight to ten feet, which would keep it out of a lot of places we could go into.

We laid out our battle order, spotted the men along the beach in firing position, and got ourselves all braced for a fracas which might end with our arrival in a Japanese prison camp or with some of us not arriving anywhere any more, ever. Finally we could make out the Japs with our night glasses. They had turned around and were heading out of the bay and keeping on around the point, until they disappeared to the south. Either they had been after us and had been baffled by the channel, in which case they would be waiting for us to stick our heads out, or else they were just making a routine inspection of all the coves and didn't know we existed.

Whichever it was we weren't going to stay there another minute. We felt as if we were smothering. A psychologist has told me since that we were having an understandable attack of galloping claustrophobia.

No matter how fast we went, the pressure of the Japs drove us faster. In moments between alarms we fed our minds with the idea that someday we would come back here and chase those Japs ten miles for every one they had chased us.

All hands piled into the boat and we got going. It wasn't too easy to do. The boards of that old dock were rotten and full of holes. Our gear was piled up there to get it out of the way while we were working on the boat. Collecting it again was a bothersome and tricky job. Something dropped through a hole in the planks, and Wolslegel cursed the darkness and Doc Head's big feet. Doc said his feet weren't big. It was almost more than Cucinello's volatile temper could endure. On temporary detached duty from us back at Bataan, he had sat alone on the deck of the steamer *Yu Sang* as a voluntary shipkeeper. The vessel was loaded with nearly a million pounds of bombs, and the Jap bombers did their best for three whole days to get him and his ship. He had calmly put out a fire started by their bombs and it hadn't raised his blood pressure, but now stumbling and fumbling around on the dock in the dark was too much for him, and Wolslegel's cursing sounded like a campfire chat compared to the pent-up words that burst from him.

We finally pushed off at slow speed, with the motor throttled down to reduce the noise, and felt our way to the channel. Just before Richardson touched the starter button, Head remarked, "The Filipinos said they were going to bring down a drum of Diesel oil for us." I pushed the remark aside.

"They've got too much trouble on their hands to be worrying about that."

But at the last minute one of them told us to stop when we got halfway out into the channel and they would bring it to us. I still didn't believe it but I said O.K., and once out there we stopped and waited. Pretty soon we heard splashing over by the beach and out they came, two of them, swimming and pushing a heavy drum of oil. It was barely floating through the water in front of them. They swam with one hand and shoved the can along with the other.

We were all pretty much on edge with the knowledge that we might find the Japs waiting to jump on us outside.

Taylor was the only one of us apparently not suffering from jittery nerves, for he kept walking from one end of the boat to the other, stumbling over us and stepping on our toes.

Finally I said, "For the love of Mike, Guns, what are you doing?"

"I'm looking for my shoes. I think I dropped them through a hole in that dock," he said. Pawing around he upset a couple of baskets of coconuts.

Dodging the Red-balls

"Good God," I said, "stop worrying about your shoes and start worrying about whether you're going to keep on living for the next few minutes or not."

He said in a hurt voice, "O.K., if that's the way you feel about it, Captain," and sat down.

When the swimmers with the oil drum were about fifty feet away, Watkins and Rankin couldn't stand waiting any longer and swam back to help them. They got into the boat and four men leaned over and lifted it in. We didn't know how to thank them. If the Japs had come in and found them helping us they would have tortured the Filipinos for days; we would have only been shot. They swam back toward shore with easy, slow strokes, and I said to the men:

"All you've got to do is to push with the poles when I say, 'Push,' and shove when I say, 'Shove,' and we'll be out of here in nothing flat."

When I gave them the word they pushed and shoved. Richardson gunned the engine when I said gun it, and we were over the coral heads and headed out into the channel. Among coral heads you can be in deep water one moment and on a reef the next, so we went slowly and took soundings with long bamboo poles. We had a couple of close scrapes and one of the coral-encrusted rocks stripped off a long white sliver of wood.

We headed out to sea, due east, away from the coast, in a gentle rain for which we were thankful since it cut down visibility. Once clear we kicked the engine wide open. We figured the Jap air- and ship-patrol lanes would only cover an area fifty miles off the coast of Mindanao and once outside this fifty-mile area our chances would be better.

I didn't know it, but all the time we had been back in that cove we must have been near a side-kick of mine, Commander Bridgett. He'd left Corregidor a week before us on a plane, together with nurses and Army and Navy officers. We got our information later on from the crew of the other plane that had started with them. Both planes had landed in a lake back in the mountains where the Army had an airfield, but in taking off from that lake Bridgett's plane had hit a rock and torn a hole in its bottom. The passengers had been disembarked and sent over to the Army camp. The next morning the Japs surrounded the lake. The plane's crew had repaired the hole in her overnight and took off at daybreak, leaving her passengers, including Bridgett, behind. Although the Japs had their own planes on the lake by this time and were swarming thickly all over the place, they were so surprised they let it get away.

Knowing Bridgett I felt sure he would have taken to the mountains rather than surrender. If we had known there was a chance he was there, we would have combed that area until we had found him or were captured ourselves.*

At midnight, I turned the tiller over to Taylor. The boat rode nicely over long, slow swells, and the dawn broke clear and fair. We could still see land on our stern but it wasn't long before even the tips of the highest peaks dropped down below the horizon.

* Recently I have seen a report in the newspapers from Japanese sources that guerrilla resistance is still being waged in Mindanao. It is my opinion (really more of a hunch than an opinion) that if such fighting is still going on, Bridgett is leading it. My only reason for thinking so is the fact that I know Bridgett and it sounds like the sort of thing he would do. Except from Jap sources, I have seen no information or intelligence out of the Philippines since I left.

Dodging the Red-balls

Chow consisted of coffee, rice with milk, raw sugar, and canned Vienna sausage, which was better to eat at sea than corned beef. Beef made you want to drink water. Whenever we had an open-sea jaunt we ate sausages. Most of us hated them. They were a kind of eye-hurting pink and when they came up out of the can they were covered with a pale coating of jelly.

I looked around at the crew that morning and realized suddenly that they weren't emaciated-looking any more. Overnight, almost, it seemed they had become tough, brown, rugged, and strong. Their beards had grown in the few days since we had left Corregidor and they had gained on an average of five to ten pounds a man. They were as satisfying a lot to have with you in a spot like ours as you could ask for.

On the previous night when we had gone to sleep we had laid out the results of our carpentry in the boat to be ready for us when we woke up, so we still had all of the braces and decking boards we had sawed the day before with us. Now the men turned to and went back to their hammering. But because of our rush in leaving, it couldn't be the work of art they had planned. They wouldn't be able to give it the combing and overlapping now to keep the job water-tight. They tried to make up for that by stretching another piece of canvas over the decking, but we didn't have any paint for the canvas. The total effect, however, was a big improvement. It increased our margin of safety, but when we picked up a wave the water still came trickling down on the sleeping men and woke them.

Binkley and I tried to figure out where the Japs would run their patrol lines in that area. Now, since they had

Mindanao, it seemed almost certain they would have an air patrol running from their big mandated island of Pelew over to Davao in Mindanao, and they would undoubtedly sight us if we tried to cross that line during the daylight hours. We checked our course and speed and discovered we would arrive at that danger spot just about daylight next morning. We could slow down, but that would keep us out in the open just so much longer. To meet the situation we cut over to the southeast. We wouldn't get away from Mindanao quite so fast but we would be well past the patrol lines when the sun came up.

We checked our improvised sextant and stowed our most accurate watch away in a wad of dry rags under the stern deck. One of the difficulties with that sextant was that when we were using it, we had to look right at the sun, with no smoked glass to protect our eyes. For minutes afterward tears streamed down our faces and whirling moons and pinwheels of light revolved dizzily between us and anything we looked at.

For the past few days the wind had blown steadily east by north. I knew that ocean currents are caused by the prevailing winds, so I figured we had about a two-knot current setting in a westerly direction. Binkley and I drew a diagram. We figured at our speed we should compensate for the current by a four-degree deviation. Just before nightfall we checked our longitude with the sunset and later with the moonrise. The night was quiet and uneventful, with a gently undulating sea. The morning was bright but not too hot and by ten o'clock we were well past the danger of being sighted by an air patrol. A few rain squalls came scurrying to us across the face of the sea, but they

Dodging the Red-balls

were isolated patches of rain and not part of any big rainstorm.

The cramped quarters were making the boys restless. Little things became matters of intense importance. We saw a school of fish jumping a few hundred yards off our beam, big fish—tuna, I think. I knew Meeker had Izaak Walton blood and asked him if he had managed to fix up any fishing lines. He brought out a couple and I took one. We fished for a while, trolling, but without much enthusiasm. I stuck at it only because the crew, grateful for any distraction, were getting a bang out of kibitzing my efforts. In the end I lost the hook and quit.

Between twilight and sunset we refueled. The sudden quiet was somehow shocking. We hadn't realized how accustomed we'd grown to the sound of the engine. Our voices sounded unnaturally loud in our ears, and we felt vaguely that something was wrong. The men could hardly wait until we started up again. Then with an engine snoring a string of fat-man snores in the stern, they relaxed.

The next day was May 21. The fresh fruit we had obtained at Leyte was still holding out. The weather was friendly, and our wake fanned out behind us, making twin lines of tumbling milk curds on the gray waste. That water was a blue-gray color, not like the deep, Caribbean blue. The men's restlessness was getting chronic and they began to crawl around the boat, driven by the irresistible desire to shift and move, even if only for a few feet. We kept our tin-can coffee urn going all day long. A cup of coffee was something to break the monotony.

Swisher had become known as "Sleeping-Sickness Swisher." When he wasn't standing watch he slept and when he got ashore he slept some more. He took a terrific needling for it but didn't seem to resent it. We didn't know he had a piece of shrapnel imbedded in his flesh and pressing against his backbone so that it hurt him when he moved. He kept buttoned up about it. At the bombing of Cavite he had been on the mine sweeper *Bittern* and had picked up his shrapnel there. He had been hospitalized for a while, but the other hospital cases had seemed so much more urgent and desperate to the surgeons that he had come back to duty on Bataan with the prodding metal still inside him. Since we needed a good engineer badly, we put in a bid and got him.

I had noticed his sleeping habits as far back as the mine-sweeping we had done when Bataan fell and had lost my temper and told him if he didn't stay awake I'd brain him.

One night while we were out in one of our boats sweeping, we had three or four mines trapped in the loop trailing out behind us when the engine fluffed out and we began to drift back right into those live mines. We sat there fascinated and helpless, like birds frozen into a trance by a snake's eyes, waiting for the rending blast that would be the last sound we'd ever hear. But Swisher got the engine going, and we pulled away just before the mines did go off. When they went it sounded as if the whole bay were one big load of TNT. First one mine went off and that one detonated two or three more. The boat jumped out of the water when the tidal wave of the concussion hit. I don't see how it missed swamping us. The whole world was one big, hideous, nerve-racking burst of sound, and I guess I blanked out for a few seconds, but when I could think again we were still afloat.

Dodging the Red-balls

After that I didn't threaten to brain Swisher for sleeping any more, and I had great respect for him. I figured that his weakness was something he couldn't help, although I didn't know what caused it.

As nearly as the doctors on the Rock could tell, the piece of shrapnel had lodged between one lung and his backbone, but they were too busy to take it out and unless he started spitting blood he was instructed to keep quiet and do nothing about it. Swisher was of Dutch extraction, with a Dutchman's capacity for stoicism, and it didn't occur to him to bellyache about it to us, because he knew there was nothing we could do about it if he did sound off.

The men were hungry for any distraction, however trivial, and I unwittingly came through with entertainment. I decided that it was about time to give my teeth a polishing. I managed to find a broken-down piece of toothbrush and filled a bailing can with water. I sat back in the after part of the boat and at first as I worked out on my upper molars it created no great stir. But the boys lost their lackluster look when I got around to my lower jaw and pulled out my false grinders, complete with plate. Newquist couldn't contain himself.

"Why, Captain," he said, with the air of a man discovering hitherto undreamed-of Shirley Temple talent in a mousy, snub-nosed daughter, "I didn't know you had store teeth."

That day is chalked up in my memory as "tooth" day. Rankin had been digging into a ripe coconut, scraping the hard white meat out of the shell with his strong, twenty-one-year-old nonstore teeth. Looking up he saw that I didn't have any coconut tidbit.

"Try this, Captain," he said. "It's the stuff."

I bit down on it, felt something snap, and a tooth fell out, one of my tailor-made pearlies. I covered the accident with my hand, threw the hunk of coconut over the side, and pretended I had lost interest in it. I didn't have to pretend very hard.

In the afternoon we spent a lot of time comparing notes on our doings at Corregidor and Bataan. Back on the *Quail* our radio man, Kenney, had rigged up a loud-speaker system so we could give the engineers down in the black hold a play-by-play account of what was going on up above from the bridge. It proved to be a good stunt psychologically, because when bombs fell near by and the concussion buckled and bent our plates inward, the boys down below could take a vicarious part in the things we were doing to the Japs in return. Meeker and Wolslegel said that they could always tell whether we were chasing the Japs or being chased. When they got the full speed bell, with no chatter over the loud-speaker, they knew that we were being attacked and doing a snake dance across the water to dodge the bombs being dumped on us. When that was going on we had no time for bomb-casting the news below, so they'd stand down there with their knees slightly bent, waiting for the jar and jolt of an explosion outside, and when it came they said they felt as though the ship was about to fall down around their ears. As soon as a stick of bombs had cracked the water open they would go around and inspect all the boilers and steam lines to see if we had sprung anything. The conversation was extremely interesting to the deck boys who had had no conception of what

Dodging the Red-balls

it meant to be down in the bowels of the ship, wondering if each moment would be the last.

When the men had used that subject up they began to work on the idea that when we got down to the Dutch East Indies and bumped into anything flying a red ball that didn't outgun us too suicidally, we ought to stand and fight and not run away any more. In the Dutch East Indies, they figured, we'd be within range of our own bombers in Australia, and they thought that the chances were if we met a Jap destroyer our bombers would keep him too busy to bother about us. So they worked on preparations to open a one-boat front. We already had the mast, boom, and sail stowed alongside, and now they worked loopholes in them through which we could stick our automatic rifles and still keep ourselves out of sight except for the man at the tiller. The idea was that the tiller man would cover himself with dirty bilge oil to make him look like a native, and that way we hoped to lure any inquisitive boat alongside before they got suspicious.

The boys got so steamed up about the idea that before very long they were discussing whether it would be better to go around looking for Jap ships to capture or take over a thinly held island and make a fortress of it. I stepped into the picture then and decided against such foolhardy belligerency. I pointed out to them that we had been away from our own forces so long we had no way of knowing what was actually afoot in the way of grand strategy, and if we raised even a small popgun commotion in that part of the world we'd be running the risk of getting the Japs all stirred up, just when our own high command in Australia might want them lulled into security.

10

Action off Longaskagawayan Point

I HAD always thought that you waited until you got to be very old and landed in a home for broken-down sailors or soldiers before you began to chew the fat about the battles you'd been in and dish up the details, no matter how small, and arguing about whether you made your attack at seven A.M. or seven-four A.M. until you got hot under the collar about it and wanted to sock somebody.

I was finding out you didn't have to wait that long. We went over the things that had happened to us back at Cavite, and on Bataan and at Corregidor, with a fine-tooth comb; checking up on each other, comparing notes, getting each moment straight, until it shaped up into a complete story.

One of our favorite themes was the action off Longaskagawayan Point, a whooper-dooper of a name any way you look at it, but I had written it in reports so many times I could toss it off one hand easy. Some of the gang thought it was the high point of the war for us.

Bird-dogging and chasing Oscars had kept up our morale after the pounding we had taken at Cavite. It was satisfying to know that we were getting war-wise and could match wits with the Japs and win a round every now and then. January was our Pickett's Charge out there. For the time being, our men on Bataan were giving the Japs a good trimming. In one frontal attack the Japs were said to have lost thirty thousand men and gained not an inch.

The rice fields of northern Bataan were covered with Japanese dead. The stench became so bad that both armies had to move their troops back away from the area. At first our boys had tried to bury the bodies, but they soon found out that all they got for their trouble was a shot from a hidden sniper. The Japanese wounded rolled over and shot our doctors who were trying to help them. We lost a lot of doctors that way before we found out this was a different kind of war from any that had gone before. Even our high-ranking Army officers were slow to acknowledge these things until they had seen them with their own eyes. I guess you have to see it and see it happen to your own countrymen before you can feel as we did. But our hatred was nothing to that of the infantrymen in the field who met the Japs face to face. They saw and smelled the beast at first hand and hated him with a cold, tempered-steel hatred.

At night the waters between Corregidor and Bataan, and between Corregidor and Caballo islands, were crowded with traffic, carrying supplies for our men in outlying forts. Some of the forts did not have their own water supply. All needed oil to keep their power plants going. All, even Bataan, drew their food supplies from the underground storehouses on Corregidor. To be stationed in the North Channel at night was like standing in a blacked-out Times Square. We were constantly afraid that the Japs might slip some of their own small boats in among the ones working for us, and one of our sweeps was anchored in the channel every night as a policeman to identify the craft as they passed. There were prearranged recognition signals, but sometimes the bone-tired officers and men from Bataan were scornful of formalities and we had to bring their boats to a stop with machine-gun fire. Occasionally we got an indignant reply, slowly spelled out, "I am Major So-and-so," or Colonel So-and-so. The *Quail* got a reputation for being a mean and hard-boiled copper, but it had to be done.

Reports began coming out of Bataan about a Jap infiltration into the hills on the seaward, or western, side. It was a serious problem, since the Japs were setting up mountain guns overlooking the main supply roads which ran up to the front lines of northern Bataan. The Army figured that it was the Navy's job to keep the Japs' sea-borne troops off the coast. For the job the Navy had Commander Bridgett, about six planeless aviators, and a few hundred sailors, collected here and there from the evacuation of Manila and Cavite. Bridgett had had command of a squadron of PBY's at the start of the war. One by one these planes were lost, after performing miracles torpedoing Jap ships.

On New Year's Eve—which none of us realized until afterward *was* New Year's Eve—with the oil tanks and everything else left at Cavite about to be blown up to prevent them from falling into the hands of the Japs who were pounding at its back door, Bridgett had come running down to the fuel dock with his men, about a hundred and fifty of them. He had been told to get back to Bataan and Mariveles by land as best he could. There were three different units of the Jap army between him and Mariveles and things didn't look too good for him. He spied a small ship slipping into the fuel dock in the gathering dusk after sunset. The ship was the *Quail*. We were getting a last bellyful of fuel. Bridgett and his men piled aboard, and we took them to Mariveles that night.

Since that time Bridgett and his officers had put together a naval battalion over at Mariveles. They had been pretty green at first and had lost some men without even seeing the Japs camouflaged in the underbrush. Bridgett fixed that by borrowing some tough old Filipino scout sergeants to give his men instruction in jungle fighting. Gradually Bridgett pushed the Jap infiltration back toward the sea until he had them all cornered on one peninsula called Longaskagawayan Point. Driving them off that point, though, was tough. The Japs had been in that area long before the war and had built secret cement gun foundations, had cached away guns and ammunition underground, and had prepared the peninsula as a possible fort for the future. They had done all this without anyone knowing it, in spite of the fact that it was government land and restricted territory. The cement in these foundations was between two and five years old.

Against this setup Bridgett couldn't do very much with his few sailor-soldiers and he reported the situation to headquarters. The Navy sent out the *Mary Anne*, a small commandeered yacht, to go around to the seaward side and take a look, but she ran into trouble. The Japs on the point opened up on her, and after they put a shot through her stack she decided it was time to get out of the way and report what she had found out.

On the night of January 29, I got a coded call on the radio to report to headquarters on Corregidor. I started over, wondering what it was all about and figuring I was being called to hear a complaint for being too hard-boiled a traffic cop in the North Channel. When I arrived at tunnel headquarters I was taken in to see the commander of the inshore patrol, Captain Hoeffel.

"Morrill, how'd you like to do a little fighting?" he wanted to know. He had a twinkle in his eye, and I was afraid he was merely kidding me.

"My God, Captain," I asked, "do you really mean it?"

"Yes," he said, "I've got a little job for you to do. I'll show you what it is."

He brought out a chart of the seaward coast of Bataan and pointed at Longaskagawayan Point.

"Commander Bridgett and our naval-battalion boys have driven the Japs out of the hills and down onto this point, but they've run into something too big for them to handle by themselves. Bridgett wants me to give him the use of a ship and I've picked the *Quail*. The Commandant and I don't like the idea of putting you on this operation because we need the *Quail* for mine sweeping and we hate to risk losing a ship. We want you to use your head up there and not let yourself get in too deep. As far as Bridgett and the Army are concerned, you'll be just a floating gun platform, but we've got other uses for you. You know what happened to the *Mary Anne* out there, so don't get in too close to their beach artillery. If you find yourself in trouble give us a priority signal on the radio. Remember that as commanding officer of your ship you are responsible for its safety, so don't let Bridgett or the Army talk you into taking any unnecessary risks."

He gave us our written orders: "At 0400 January 29 you will proceed through the inner mine field and pick up Commander Bridgett and his party at Mariveles. Proceed from then on in accordance with his verbal instructions."

The Captain wished us good luck then, and I walked out of the tunnel, feeling pretty good. As I crossed over the hump at the base of Malinta Hill and on over to the north dock where my boat was waiting, I thought of ways and means to make the expedition a success. The Voice of Freedom, Corregidor's little local radio, was just signing off as I passed by the entrance to the big Army tunnel. They always finished with the *Star-Spangled Banner*, and I remember thinking that of all the war songs that hundred-year-old anthem had them all beat as a spine-stiffener. At least it did to us out there.

I decided not to say anything to our other officers and crew that night. Usually when we had been given some special job to pull off I called them together and mapped it out for them, but there are plenty of people who don't sleep well when they think there is a good chance they may not live through the next day, and they needed all the sleep they could get.

There was plenty to do in the morning. Taylor, our gunnery officer, had gone to the hospital two days before. Lee, our executive officer and second in command, could have been very helpful to me on the bridge, but I didn't want him up there. I wanted him as far away from me as possible, back aft at the after steering station, so that if something happened to me there would be someone left to pull the ship out of the hole.

With Taylor and Lee counted out there was no one else on the ship except myself who knew enough about gunnery to control the firing. We had two chief quartermasters who were qualified to handle the control of the ship's steering and navigation. We ended up with a rather unusual combination on the bridge. I acted as gunnery officer and Byrd, our chief gunnery officer, acted as captain. I told him where I wanted the ship to be and he and his gang did all the piloting and steering. These arrangements seemed to baffle the Army officers who took the trip with us, and they finally asked me, "Who the hell is captain of this ship anyway?" But outside of disturbing the Army's sense of the fitness of things, the arrangement worked out fine.

There were other things to arrange. We had to strike up extra quantities of the type of ammunition used for firing at surface targets, since most of our work in the past had been antiaircraft work. There had to be a special arrangement of our fire-control telephones. One earphone was connected with the gun firing at the beach and the other phone had to be connected to the other three-inch gun and the machine guns that were to keep the planes off our necks. A single switch permitted me to talk to the two groups of gunners separately, while I could listen to all the guns all the time. There were extra crow's-nest lookouts to post on the chance that Jap naval vessels would try to sneak up on us. We wanted to be sure to see them first as our gun power was a lot better for fighting off air attack

Action off Longaskagawayan Point

than it was for shooting it out with big ships. We put our best lookout, Binkley, up there and connected him up with a special telephone hookup which included the large searchlights.

Bridgett was waiting for us at Mariveles in a small motorboat with Major Pugh and several other Army officers. We started through the outer mine field. The night was pitch-black. There was no moon and, of course, no navigational lights marking the channel, so we had to take our bearings on the hazy outlines of the islands. That particular mine field was one of our Army fields and had live mines in it that were plenty big. The channel through it was only two hundred yards wide, and we scraped the unlighted mine-field marker buoy at the end of the channel. It was that close.

Once clear of the mine field, Bridgett and I went into the lightproof cabin to talk over our plan of operations from his angle. Bridgett explained that his ground troops were holding a line across the ridge at the base of Longaskagawayan Point. The point was shaped like a razor-backed hog, with the snout sticking out to seaward. The sides and seaward ends of the point were honeycombed with caves and natural hideouts. Scrub brush and small trees grew in scattered clumps on the sides, thickest along the water's edge. The Japs had their artillery pieces hidden there. At seven-thirty in the morning a battery of big mortars from Corregidor was going to open up on the top ridge and south side of the point. Another battery of our Army seventy-fives was to open up at the same time from a point farther up the coast and cover the north side of the point. Our job was to polish off the seaward end and seek out the hard spots of resistance. By means of a special radio-telephone circuit Bridgett was to control the whole show from his vantage point on our bridge.

"We've got to do the job in a hurry," he said. "By tomorrow morning at the latest. The Japs on the point are being reinforced each night by sea from their submarines and surface vessels and they are getting tougher to crack every day. They have already set up their artillery to blast our supply roads to our front lines on Bataan."

I asked him where he wanted the *Quail* to be when the show began.

"I want the *Quail* to be as close to shore as you can get her. I need visibility to control the Army gunfire and I want to be in there where I can see our ground forces coming down the ridge."

When he mentioned the close-range idea, I told him about our instructions.

"The hell with that!" he exploded. "You're in command now. What're you going to do?"

"Take it easy," I told him. "We'll be in there plenty close enough to suit you when things start popping."

We went over the whole thing once more and then shifted back to the bridge. We had been there only a moment when our Army searchlights along the Corregidor shore, thinking we looked suspicious, opened up on us with the full power of their stabbing shafts of light. The intense brilliance made us feel stripped and bare.

Bridgett blew up with a loud pop. He grabbed the bridge extension of our radio telephone and called the Army station.

"This is Bridgett calling," he bellowed. "Get those God-damned searchlights off of us right away. If you don't turn 'em off by the time I stop talking I'll come over there after you."

He used code words for his various stations. The station he was calling happened to be "Purple." The answer to his message came back:

"Purple to Bridgett. Message understood."

It was a wonder that Purple didn't hear Bridgett without benefit of earphones.

"To hell with whether you understand or not. Get those searchlights off of us."

He turned to me. "What do you think of that?" he asked. "I personally told each searchlight group not to open up on us under any circumstances and to expect us to be here at this time."

I picked up a cup of coffee and handed it to him. "The Japs won't know what to make of it either," I said. "It's so screwball they'll probably think we're one of their own ships."

"God damn it, Morrill," he said, "I don't know how you keep your temper. I guess you're not as Irish as I am."

He had an Irish face and dark hair. He was heavy-set and high-strung but he had plenty of guts.

The lights went out, and we kept on our northerly course for fifteen minutes more. Then we got a second surprise package from the shore. A group of our own fifty-caliber machine guns began to blast away at us. They were pretty far away and we couldn't hear their sound, but we could see the bright pink glow of their tracer bullets as they passed ahead and above us. We couldn't blame the gunners ashore. The Japs had been sending in supplies under cover of darkness, and our beach-defense men were on edge. From their point of view they were perfectly justified in shooting at any unidentified objects they could make out, out there in the darkness. We couldn't stop them since we had no telephonic communication with them.

Bridgett was exasperated all over again. "We'd better head out to sea and get out of their range and come back off the point at the appointed time. We'll have to run at full speed, but we'll just about make it," I said.

"O.K.," he told me, "and by the way my name is Frank."

"O.K., Frank," I said.

At the end of another fifteen-minute run, the lookouts in the crow's-nest reported something that looked like a Jap cruiser close aboard on our starboard bow. We veered away, and I sounded the general alarm for action stations. Meanwhile I examined the shadowy shape through the night glasses. It turned out to be our own patrol vessel, the *Mary Anne*, and we exchanged recognition signals. I found out later that Captain Hoeffel had sent her out there to be on hand in the morning to pick up possible survivors from the *Quail*. Evidently he hadn't thought our chances were too good.

We arrived off the point just as the dawn began to drain the ink out of the sky over Mariveles to the eastward. Edging in slowly we arrived three thousand yards away at seven-twenty-seven. If you've ever watched the sun rise at sea you've noticed that in the east, where the sun is going to come up, the sky is a light color and objects to the eastward of you stand out clearly, but toward the west it is still dark and it is hard to see anything over there until

Action off Longaskagawayan Point

much later. We were approaching from the westward and it kept us hidden from the Japs on the point until time for us to go into action.

Sharp on the dot of seven-thirty the first salvo of heavy twelve-inch shells from the Corregidor mortars landed in the water between us and the point. We could see them splash in the water before they cracked the morning quiet wide open with the whe-e-e-ing noise they made traveling through the air.

Using his special radio-telephone circuit Bridgett gave Corregidor a spot telling them "Right 200."

While we waited for the next salvo, the first bursts from our seventy-five battery landed squarely on the north slope of the point.

"Hit. No change. North battery," Bridgett said on the telephone.

Meanwhile, as we had planned it, Byrd (our chief gunnery officer, now acting as captain) was zigging the *Quail* and closing in on the point. We hoped the Japs' hidden field guns would open fire on us so that we could see their positions. The second salvo from Corregidor's battery landed squarely and Bridgett didn't have to give the mortars any more instructions. Once the shells started popping, Bridgett was much happier. Turning to me he said, "You can open fire any time you're ready."

Major Pugh helped me pick out a cave on the ocean end of the point as our target and we opened up with one gun. Our second shot hit where we wanted it to. The Japs didn't wait for more nudging and opened up with two field-artillery pieces along the southern edge of the point down low near the water line. They were cleverly camouflaged, but their flashes of smoke gave them away. We shifted our aim to the nearest Jap battery and scored a square hit with our next two-gun salvo. The Japs sent misses off our port beam five hundred feet away. They were having trouble adapting their army fieldpieces to our rapid zigging. Another of our two-gun salvos polished off a second Jap fieldpiece and sent dark fragments flying through the air. It would have been good shooting in any league and I was proud of it, but I tried not to let Pugh and Bridgett see how tickled I was.

After that there was no more enemy fire. During the next hour we closed in to four hundred yards and then to nine hundred. It was as close as we could get without ramming the *Quail* on the rocks. We systematically sprayed every nook, cranny, cave, and clump of trees with shells. Major Pugh and his party coached me on likely spots where they had seen the Japs taking cover. It was a big help having them aboard, as they knew their land warfare. What to us looked like a dirty clump of bushes would prove to be a heavy machine-gun nest when we touched it up with a three-inch shell under the Major's prompting.

In the meantime our ground forces were waiting until we had finished mopping up. The hunk of volcanic rock and green growth on which we had the Japs cornered began to lose shape and contour, like a craggy, pockmarked face going slack.

In about half an hour Bridgett told the heavy mortars to cease fire since we didn't want to waste any more big shells, but the *Quail*'s three-inchers continued to pump lead into that messed-up patch of ground a little longer. Dirt spurted under the hammering thrusts of the hell we were sending over, and powder fumes drifted up from our guns and stung the lining of our nostrils and throats.

At eight o'clock a radio dispatch from headquarters told us that a Jap cruiser of the *Idzuma* type was bearing down in our direction about twelve miles away. Headquarters wanted to know if we saw it. We didn't see it for fifteen minutes. Then our crow's-nest made it out, hull-down on the horizon, but by that time I was a lot more interested in a formation of nine Jap dive bombers which appeared in the blue to the north of us. Using our split gun control we kept on pecking away at the shore with one gun and readied the other one to beat off an air attack. The dive bombers came close enough for us to open up on them and we gave them a few bursts, but they didn't peel out of formation and zoom down at us. Instead, they delivered their attack on the other side of the hill on our supply highway running up into Bataan. As usual, they had orders to do just what they were doing and wouldn't adapt themselves to a new set of circumstances, even when they saw us and felt the lifting jar of our antiaircraft under them.

Adding the appearance of the cruiser to that of the dive bombers, it seemed a good guess that the Japs had decided to start a combined air, sea, and land operation on that particular morning, but as far as troops and the battery on that point were concerned, we had taken care of the land part of it.

At eight-thirty another radio dispatch came from headquarters: "Are you in danger from Jap cruisers?" We sent back a negative, explaining that as far as we were concerned the cruiser was an old-type can with ineffective gunpowder. But headquarters kept right on worrying about us and whipped out another message: "Return at discretion." We didn't take time out to reply to that one and continued working.

Bridgett gave the walky-talky man with the ground forces the word to advance. We provided a rolling barrage with both of our guns. At times this barrage came very close to our own troops and Bridgett asked the walky-talky man, "How was that last burst?"

"Too good," the walky-talky man said. "It bounced right off the commanding officer's foot. Move it down a little before you knock the beard off his chin."

The advance continued and, amazingly enough, we took over the point without a single casualty to our troops.

At ten minutes to nine, headquarters decided they had been patient enough with us and gave us a "Return to port."

I asked Bridgett if he were all finished and he said, "Give me just a few more minutes."

I acted on the letter of headquarters' orders, if not the spirit, and swung the ship around in a large circle and continued firing until Bridgett was ready to call it a day. Headquarters was getting peeved at us now and asked testily, "Are you returning?" Figuring Captain Hoeffel was probably having a cat fit, I headed the ship southward for the return. Nothing much happened on the trip back except for one threatened dive-bombing attack, and I was glad it was comparatively quiet because our guns were so hot the paint was peeling from them in flakes and strips.

As we neared our anchorage, headquarters ordered Bridgett and myself to report immediately. We looked at each other and said, "I guess we're in for it now. They'll

Action off Longaskagawayan Point

be tipping us the black spot." Later on we found out through the grapevine that at the very least we had been in for a good lacing from our boss, but five minutes before we reached the headquarters tunnel, General Wainwright had called him up and congratulated him on what he called "an amazing series of operations and extremely satisfactory co-operation between the two branches of the service," and so we were well met.

There was some huffing and puffing, but in the end the Commandant and Captain Hoeffel were swell about it.

We found out later that of the four hundred Japs on the point three hundred and ninety-five of them had died rather than surrender. There were no wounded. Two of them had jumped off the cliff and three were captured in the water.

Months later, out there in a little thirty-six-foot boat we felt very much like that ourselves. There hadn't been any bravado or belligerent ranting about it, but almost without discussing it we had made up our minds that nobody would take us alive either.

11

Through the Indies

By the time we had finished fueling it was already black in the east and we had just a few more minutes in which to catch a last cigarette before the long cigaretteless night watches. Doc Head reached into his locker beneath the sea boards and fumbled among his "miracle bags." For days now we had watched him produce bandages, tape, merthiolate, cigarettes, or one of his own gooey medical concoctions from them. This time he put on a long face and announced there was just one cigarette apiece left. He had had us on slim smoke rations for a week or more, but we hadn't really believed in his "Better go easy, boys," talk. We smoked our last cigarette, trying to drag a little extra pleasure out of it, but it tasted just like any other cigarette. We had our final drag just as the blackness of a moonless night closed in upon us. A scattering of stars shone overhead through breaks in the dark stratus clouds. They twinkled for a few minutes, a light wind drove the clouds across them, and they went out. Sometimes a little bank of clouds would stay in one spot long enough for us to use it as a course marker, but more often than not the clouds would deceive us and we'd find ourselves off our course. The same thing happened when we tried to watch the ocean swells and gauge our course by them. There was no alternative but to use the compass, so we cut a tiny hole in the hood over the compass and peered through it. But we didn't like the idea. We felt that little pinprick of light illuminated us like a Christmas tree.

We brought out three or four bananas for the night watch. We were banana specialists by this time and bought them in various stages of greenness so that some of them would be ripe today, others tomorrow, and still others a week later. But even better for night watches than bananas were the limes we had bought in Leyte. The men found that when they sucked on one it took their minds off cigarettes.

Haley called me in the morning, and I found that we were off the northeast coast of Morotai. Morotai was a pretty good-sized island, sixty miles long. We had heard that there were no Japs on Morotai or on the group of islands directly to the south of us. The question now was whether to make a beach on the windward side through the surf or go around to leeward. In order to save time and distance we decided to tackle the surf. The surf wasn't a high one, the sea only broke three or four feet over the reef, but we couldn't see any break in it. To climb over a reef in a motorized boat is quite a thing. You don't know what you're going to hit on the other side. You might land squarely on coral heads or split your bottom wide open in shallow water only six inches deep. The smart thing was to avoid the surf, with our heavily laden boat.

We ran for two hours looking for a break before we gave up and went ahead and had breakfast.

In the middle of breakfast Taylor said, "If that ain't a red-ball flag I don't know what it is."

It brought us all up with a bang, rice and raw sugar stuck halfway down our throats. The crew ducked down, and I got out the glasses. Sure enough, there was a forty-foot Jap steam launch with a Jap merchant flag on it. It had just come out of a cove and was running along inside of the reef, parallel to us.

It was doubtful if they saw us. We were a mile and a half away and low in the water, but it did change our mind about making a landing, and we headed out to sea and kept going. The crew had manned their battle stations and were squinting along their gun barrels through the loopholes. Steele, the fire-eater, said, "We ought to take that monkey over."

But I didn't figure it was as good a boat as ours, even if we had been able to give it the business. From then on for the rest of the day we worried about whether it had sighted us and had radioed the news to one of its air bases. It didn't seem likely that a boat that small would have a radio but we couldn't be sure, and possibly the Japs might have had a radio set up on the beach in a lookout station or a tower, so we busily read the sky for planes.

It was hot as the hinges of hell under the decking, and we stewed and panted down there until around two o'clock when we crossed an open stretch of water and felt relatively safe.

Five o'clock found us off the northeast coast of Halmahera, headed south. We ran through schools of big fish jumping two or three feet out of the water, twisting their tails and trying to play games with our boat, but we were too slow for them and they grew disgusted and went away.

Since it was late afternoon there was no point in going ashore. Nighttime was the time for us to do our traveling. Our experience with the Jap red-ball had made us cautious about landing on any of the Dutch East Indies islands.

But for three solid days we had been so cramped that the confinement was beginning to make us cranky, so I combed the chart for a tiny island too insignificant for the Japs to notice.

"Maybe we can find some corn silk and we can smoke," Clarke said wistfully.

I picked out a little island just off the coast of Halmahera, sixty miles to the south, figuring we could reach it by morning. Its name was Sajafi. The men complained that the natives ought to put up signs on their islands with a name on it to make it easier for us, like, "You are now entering Sajafi, hell-hole of the southern Pacific. The Lions Club meets every Tuesday at the Coconut Inn."

Before the sun went down I showed Taylor the chart and the whole setup and warned him about the danger of overshooting Sajafi because of our greater speed. I told him if he got there before morning to lie to and wait for daybreak.

I slept like a log. The next thing I knew he was leaning over me, saying, "I think you'd better get up." I got up like a shot; for one confused moment I imagined we were back at Corregidor and that the Japs were coming up our tunnel.

Taylor said, "But there's an extra-heavy rain squall moving over toward us and I wanted you to see the island on our port before the squall blanks it out. We've been lying to here since one o'clock."

The island was less than half a mile away, resting on the inverted bowl of the sea. It was low and flat. It had one hill about fifty feet high, covered with coconut and hardwood trees, and we were on its leeward side where we wanted to be.

"Are you sure it's Sajafi?" I asked him.

"Hell, no," he said. "Sajafi or Long Island, it looks all the same to me. I just did what you told me to, and stopped when we came to an island on our port."

"Whatever it is, it'll do," I said.

I told Stringer to get the engine started so we could run in and anchor there until daylight. As we started, the rain squall reached the island and blotted it out. Then it reached us, and for a few moments it was as if firemen were playing a hose on us. I had Clarke take a sounding with our improvised lead line, found it was shallow enough to anchor, and we dropped our hook. No sooner had we done that than the rain passed as quickly as it had arrived. There were light-gray streaks in the east and in a few more minutes day was coming on fast. We got the anchor up and headed in. Taylor was up in the bow guiding us through the coral heads and reefs, his arms wigwagging signals to us. But the going was too difficult and we went back on out. By that time we spied native canoes, looking like Filipino bancas, a quarter of a mile to the south and native huts fringing the beach.

We went down and turned in where the boat was able

to get up on the beach on a sandy bottom, fifty feet from shore, and we could wade the rest of the way in.

We sent Head and Swisher pushing through the wavelets lapping along the beach, to find out what the situation was and let us know before we lugged our camp gear ashore. Swisher claimed to be able to speak Dutch, and we thought that might help. I tried to get the Doc to take a pistol with him, but he said he had no use for one.

"If they're going to shoot me, they're going to shoot me. I couldn't hit anything with a pistol anyway." He took all his clothes off and carried them over his head. We yelled after him, "You'll scare 'em all to death before you get there, Doc." But he didn't stop, and when he reached the beach he calmly put his clothes back on. Our ambassadors stood there for some time talking to the natives or trying to. Swisher didn't seem to be saying much, in spite of his boasted Dutch, but Doc was waving his arms and making sweeping motions. We yelled over, "What do they say, Swisher?"

"You got me," he yelled back.

"Well, talk Dutch to 'em."

"These jerks don't even know their own language. They don't even know Tagalog."

"Talk Moro to them."

But that was no good either. "They don't even know Moro," Swisher shouted.

Head was making out better. At least they were nodding to him.

"Doc, what's the dope?" we called.

"It's O.K.," he yelled. "I'm trading my drawers for a load of coconuts."

"Boy, are they getting gypped!" someone yelled back.

We wondered where Doc had got them. None of the rest of us had any underwear.

"That Doc's got everything," Cucinello said. "If we only knew the truth he's probably got a blonde in those duffel bags of his."

I jumped into the water and went up to Head to find out how he was making out. He said he was making out fine.

"All I need is to be left alone," he said.

I stood there watching him, fascinated. He waved his arms around and drew pictures in the sand with a stick. He claimed he had already swapped a hundred coconuts and was just trying to get them to understand the word banana.

"What word are you using for banana?" I asked him.

He said he was using the word banana. "What other word would I use?" he asked testily.

His system seemed to be to try to sell them an idea twenty-five times. If it didn't work he kept on going. Along about the fiftieth time they'd get it. After he put over the banana idea he went into a papaya campaign. It was comical to watch but it worked. About the only thing they wanted from us were clothes, which was the only thing we didn't have enough of, but we traded them what we could spare and worked in some gauze rolls and a few odds and ends of spare medical supplies. These natives were as black as tar and had no resemblance to Filipinos, the Moros, or any tribe we had ever seen. They wore rough, cotton, unbleached drawers which the Dutch had supplied them with, and nothing above the waist at all.

Through the Indies 189

They were taller and better built than the Moros, but the Moros were browner, while these men were African in type.

Meeker started breakfast, and by this time Head was trying for tobacco. They didn't grow it themselves and were short of it but we finally did get some. Head was so busy he forgot about breakfast.

"I'll talk to 'em awhile," I said, "you slip over and get something to eat."

Using Head's system I tried to find out the name of the island. I pointed to the ground and said, "What's this?" The old chief must have thought I meant sand, for he gave me a word that meant nothing to me. I pointed to Halmahera off in the distance, then back to the island again.

They said, "Sajafi."

I pointed to myself and said, "What am I?"

They said, "American."

Head swore he hadn't told them the word. Maybe we just smelled American to them.

Head kept them entertained the rest of the afternoon while the rest of us slept. He found out some pretty useful things that way—a well where we could get fresh water and a place where we could bathe. Only the bathing wasn't much good because in the creek they sent us to were crocodiles six feet long.

In the evening we shoved off, pretending we were headed toward Halmahera. After dark, we cut southeast to approach the coast of New Guinea. The chart showed lots of shoal areas there and we had heard that the island of Ceram, just south, had Japs on it. We wanted to stay away from the larger islands and jump from one small one to another.

That night we headed across Jilolo Strait for the island of Gagi.

The current set us back and we arrived off Gagi at daybreak. We changed our minds about stopping at Gagi before we got there, deciding that its position and size might make it a Jap outpost. Before it was light enough for us to be seen, we swerved to the right and were seven miles east of it by sunup. Then we went south again and headed for a little group of islands small enough not to attract sea traffic, called the Jeff family group. Just as we turned south, Steele picked up a peculiar object to eastward through the glasses. We could see the heads of six or eight men apparently walking through the water up to their necks, an illusion caused by the fact that their boat was hull down to us. When the boat came up into sight over the horizon we could see it was a power-driven launch going north. We headed almost due west for a mile or so and lost it. After another mile we picked up another one and we used the same maneuver.

Reaching the outboard island of the Jeff family group we picked a deserted island, a small one with no underbrush, just trees, so low-lying that during storms seas had washed right over it. It was a rocky outcropping in the water with no beach, and since there was no beach it was laborious work getting our supplies across the submerged rocks, but once ashore it was swell. We just lay around and rested.

The night before, we had crossed the equator, but feeling that we had more important things on our mind than horseplay or initiations by Neptune's court I hadn't told the boys about it until now. It seemed to make a big impression on them. It was obvious that the news meant to

Through the Indies

them that we were on the home stretch. They all began to feel cocky, as though the trip were in the bag and as if, as far as they were concerned, we had dropped right through a hole in the bottom of Hirohito's pocket. They became even more chart-conscious, tried to figure out how much farther we had to go, and told Binkley to keep a colorful log of our experiences.

"We don't want to forget where we've been and the times we've skizzled the Nips. We want to be able to tell the folks all about it when we get home," they said.

Binkley promised to keep a log full of provocative details, but when I looked at it from time to time it read just like any ship's log, full of stuff about the tides, number of knots, and what we had for chow, and that was about all.

Some of us had developed tropical ulcers. They started with almost any abrasion. An insect bite or a scratch would do it. We found out later from the doctors in Australia that such sores were very prevalent in that part of the world and no one had ever found a satisfactory cure for them.

Binkley went out to the boat to get the chart and came back stumbling, and splashing, with the chart held high over his head to keep it dry. We spread it out and made a circle around it. Wolslegel suggested, as he usually did, that we head south and keep going without a stop until we reached our destination. He was the restless one of our party. We asked him if he had a date in Australia, but he merely said, "I'm tired of fooling around." Maybe his tropical ulcers had something to do with it. He had them worse than anyone else.

Most of the others found themselves wishing we didn't

have to go through all of the things we were going through. It was too bad we couldn't pause here and there to savor the trip.

By that time a sense of adventure had pervaded our consciousness. We knew that probably never again in our lives would we live quite as fully, be quite as self-sufficient, or be quite as independent of the things we call civilization. We were eighteen men alone in a vast and lonesome world. But that world was intensely interesting. None of us knew quite how to express it.

We all felt that some power, stronger than circumstance, had been looking out for us. It wasn't possible that so many coincidences could have been luck and luck alone. We remembered how the *Quail* had survived those last days of continuous bombing lying there immobile, with dead boilers and no oil. Why the Japs hadn't sunk her and why they hadn't even so much as scratched one of our men was a mystery to us. But we did know that except for the *Quail* being afloat that last night in Corregidor we would have all been trapped there too.

Then, too, if it hadn't been for that mine-sweeping job, we wouldn't have had the boats scattered and loaded with Diesel oil. That last night the Commandant had wanted us to stay in the tunnel and rest, but most of the men had chosen to sleep on the ship. And it was while we were all out there, out on the ship working, instead of resting in the tunnel, that the Japs had chosen an hour out of all the hours to make their final attack. Afterward we had been sent to work in the one fort that didn't surrender when the others did. There was no real reason why we should have lived through that job of scuttling the *Quail*. It was

Through the Indies

impossible that we had. Anyone could see that it was sure death. Escaping through those Jap picket boats seemed much less to us somehow. The biggest miracle of all had been in getting away from Corregidor. It was almost as if when we had a problem or a situation to meet, we had only to open our minds and the right solution would flow in.

We went back in our minds to the bombing of Cavite Navy Yard and lived it over again, and I found myself gassing away with the best of them. Some of the gang asked me how it had been for me at Cavite, and I told them. I wanted to see if it was straight in my mind and I asked them to keep tabs on me as I went along, to see that I had it right.

At three o'clock in the morning of December 8 in Cavite —midmorning in Hawaii—the lights on the *Quail* had gone out. It was no ordinary practice blackout—even dock power to ships at the wharfs was cut off. Fans and blowers slowed down and stopped. The sudden silence woke me up. Still fuzzy with sleep, I rolled out, slipped on a pair of pants, and went down to the *Quail*'s main deck to ask the gangway watch what was up. He was bending over a slip of paper, using a tiny pin point of a flashlight.

Turning, he handed me the paper. It said in big capital letters: JAPAN HAS COMMENCED HOSTILITIES. GOVERN YOURSELF ACCORDINGLY.

I said, "Call all hands." Some of the urgency must have jumped from that paper into my voice, for Wilson moved faster than he had ever done in all the time I had known him, and he had never been a slowpoke.

There had been plenty of alerts before, and we thought we were letter perfect and smooth as silk in the drills we had had. But the real thing caught us in the final stages of what had been a hasty Navy Yard overhaul. It had been hasty because even the bootblacks in the Manila barbershops knew a storm was blowing up and it was only a matter of when it would break. We had hoped we could slip out of the yard before it broke, but it had caught us with a week to go before the yard would call our overhaul job complete. We felt in our bones that Cavite was in for a pasting, and that old Spanish-built yard with its antiquated buildings would burn like a pile of celluloid shavings.

What could we do? First of all, we needed ammunition. We had only a little aboard. Having it aboard during the welding operations of a yard overhaul is a dangerous fire hazard, and the rest was stowed in the ammunition depot, some distance away. It would take time to get that ammunition, and we wanted it in a hurry: by daybreak—the most likely time for an air attack. We got it from the *Finch*, a sister ship, and stowed it away in record time. Parts of our engines were still in the shop and the next problem was how to get the ship away from a burning Cavite—if it burned.

The *Finch* slipped away and left the *Pigeon* and the *Quail* sitting there. We didn't blame her. The *Pigeon* was under repairs too, and both of us were lame ducks, but the *Finch* had done all she could do for us before reporting for duty in the outer harbor.

Dick Hawes was the skipper of the *Pigeon* and Dick never lacked ideas. We had one set of engines between the two of us but no rudders. That is, the *Pigeon* could use her engine if she absolutely had to, but neither of us had a rudder. We decided that at the first warning of bombers we'd cut our lines loose from the dock and drift away to a safe distance, using Dick's engines and the tidal current to push us.

The way it worked out we had better luck than that. We were given a whole day and a half of grace before the Nips struck. We could and did do a hell of a lot in the next forty-eight hours. But we kept our basic plan on tap in the back of our heads.

The morning of December 10 found us in better shape. The Filipino yard workmen had stuck to their posts without a break, not even leaving to find out whether or not their families were being taken care of. They had forgotten the eight-hour day. The workday now had twenty-four hours in it or more. In some cases the yard workmen dropped beside their lathes, out on their feet, from exhaustion. We knew because we followed each nut and bolt, valve and piston, from one shop to the next. We saw workmen, both white and brown, seize a piece of material from one machine and run with it to another to save a vital second.

A few hours later we were to see those same workmen piled high in great heaps in their machine shops—the dead killed by the first bombs piled high on trucks—while lying silent around them in strange twisted positions were other workmen who had been about to trundle out their stricken companions when the second wave of bombs struck them down, too.

There were some bits of grim satisfaction in those hectic last hours of Cavite. Red tape went by the board. To our surprise, we found we could draw additional ammunition without signing reams of papers and waiting for the necessary signatures. The same held true for supplies and provisions of all sorts. We took advantage of it and it helped us hold on in the months to come.

There were a number of other ships in the yard, but we were so engrossed in our own problems we were hardly conscious of them. We were still nested together with the *Pigeon*, but now our engines were turning over slowly alongside the dock in our final dock trial, which is the last thing a ship under repair undergoes before leaving a yard.

By this time we had the use of our rudder, but the repairs on the *Pigeon*'s steering gear still hadn't been finished. The extra ammunition and supplies had been pouring aboard all morning, and Dick Hawes and I sat down to a midday snack of lunch with a feeling of relief. We had barely touched our chairs, however, when the general-alarm howler went off with a shriek. The warning howler always has an eerie sound, but from this time on and for many days to come it was to mean sheer terror.

A man thinks of a thousand things while he is racing for his general quarters station. I know I did. I guess you work your fears out that way, for I have never seen a man shake while he was in action, but I've seen plenty go into a jitter routine at the first blast of that deadly howler. When he is new at the game, and hears it for the first time, the blood drains from a man's face.

And being new at the game means a long time for most. Along about the twentieth action you either get a fatalistic attitude or crack up and can't take it any more.

We raced for our stations that noon of December 10 with our food untasted. We could see the Japs all right.

There were fifty-four coming over in neat, precise formations with unmistakable red balls on their wings. Previously, I had heard our senior officers worrying more about their fear that we might fire on our own planes than about our not firing at the Japs, and I was dope enough to wonder for one fleeting instant whether or not we'd be given permission to fire. But there was no time to wonder. We just fired, permission or not. With our guns all whanging away and under Taylor's control, my next thought was about moving the ship. I glanced over at Dick Hawes, but his guns were blazing away too, and it was impossible to shout to him or send him a message by signaling. There was too much noise and flame from our own guns right under our noses.

We used a few arm motions on each other and got our ideas across—somehow he got his men to cut loose the *Pigeon*'s lines in the midst of all that confusion. We kept the lines between the *Pigeon* and the *Quail* so that the *Pigeon* could stay tied to us and take advantage of our rudder control. Our engine was still turning over on its dock trial when I rang for "Full speed astern." I hoped the boys down below would know it was the real thing and not just a mistaken dock-trial signal.

They probably thought I was nuts, but they gave me the benefit of the doubt and we got the hell out of there in nothing flat, with the *Pigeon* right along with us, helping us with her engine. As we rounded Machina wharf, the huge bulk of the tender *Otis* blanked off our fire for a few minutes and with our guns silent we could see we were going a little better. A gunboat—which one I'll never know—was right across our path, trying to maneuver out of the narrow channel. We dodged her by first backing our engine and then the *Pigeon*'s, then giving both full speed ahead until we squeezed in between the gunboat and the *Otis*, with inches to spare.

In the meantime the *Otis* was starting to move away from her dock, which didn't help make our path an open seaway. She was none too soon. A bomb opened up her stern. It was our first experience with a bomb close at hand, but we didn't have time to brood about it long, for another tore up the water just astern of us and spurred us on.

Dick and I asked our engines for all they had. We wanted to reach the open water of Canacao Bay where we could do a little dodging and get our guns in position to go to town on the Japs.

When we made it we split up. Then racing around in circles, we cut loose at the Jap planes. It would be swell if I could say that we put in some good licks on them that day. But we had a lot to learn about warfare. We had been proud of ourselves in our target practices before the war. We weren't proud now. All of our carefully worked-out systems of firing against planes didn't amount to a hill of beans.

In the first place, the planes were too high. In the second place, there weren't just one or two planes coming at us. They came in droves—and from every direction. We concentrated on a group and tracked them in, only to have them swerve off and go after another target. Meanwhile a group that hadn't been bothering us dropped racks of eggs on us. To top it all off, before the Japs were halfway through with us, we began to run short of ammunition. Later on we learned how to correct the mistakes we made that day. We learned to play dumb as a fox and hold our fire until it counted. Before we were finished with them the Japs learned that even small mine sweepers could bite. But this time we were just duckpins set up in an alley for them. Target practices were all right, but war is a business and we had to learn the tricks of the trade the hard way before we were any good at it.

When three o'clock in the afternoon rolled around, the Nip planes finally shoved off and disappeared. They'd been at it for three hours, and the Cavite Navy Yard was a blazing wreck. The sudden cessation of firing left us limp. We slowed down our engines and started to head back toward the yard, wondering what was next.

Our first thought was, we were homeless. Next of all we asked ourselves, "Where is the division commander?"

We were afraid to think what had happened to him as we had last seen him ashore in the yard. He turned up safe later, but for the moment we were bossless as well as homeless.

The *Whippoorwill* came steaming by from seaward where she had been mine sweeping. And her skipper, Thug Ferriter, asked me by signal, "Shall I try to put out the fires in the yard?"

The idea was preposterous. We could no more have doused those leaping flames than we could have extinguished Vesuvius. But it snapped me out of our daze with a bang. For the first time the thought hit me, how about the subs and destroyers that were in the yard when we left? A quick glance told me they hadn't got out. I started to send a signal to Thug and Dick Hawes, but it was unnecessary. The same idea had hit them at the same time, and they were already headed in. Thug was in the lead. His ship went in for the *Perry*, one of our World War destroyers. She was badly hit and the dock alongside her was blazing. Thug had one hell of a time getting her out. The channel was filled with wreckage, and the *Whip* and the *Perry* got so twisted and snarled together they looked like steel pretzels.

The *Perry* caught on fire. The lines Thug put aboard her burned almost as fast as he could send them over. Ammunition was exploding almost constantly, but somehow Thug got those fires out and snaked the *Perry* away from the blazing dock. It was a miracle of seamanship and good organization by Thug and his crew. The *Pigeon* was hauling out a sub and blocking our path so that we couldn't do anything for a few minutes, and we had a grandstand view of it. The *Pigeon* had her difficulties, too. Over where she lay (Machina wharf), the torpedoes in the torpedo shop on the wharf were exploding. They were really something to put a kink in your spine. When one of them went off, whole sides of buildings sailed right over the *Pigeon* like huge black birds. But in spite of everything, the *Pigeon* got her sub out. That left the *Bittern* (one of our sister ships) and an ammunition lighter loaded with aviation torpedoes left behind at the dock where the sub had been.

The *Bittern* was badly holed by shrapnel fragments but she was intact otherwise. Our choice lay between her and the lighter. I suppose the lighter was the more valuable as far as the war effort was concerned. Anyhow, with the aid of a motor launch and the more than brave *Bittern* crew, we managed to get both out before the torpedo shop blew up completely.

Through the Indies

The *Bittern* was in bad shape. Even a landlubber could see she would be out of commission for a long time to come, so we took her crew on board the *Quail*. We kept a good many of them for the rest of the war, and they were a big help. As a matter of fact, three of our final eighteen wanderers were ex-*Bittern* men—Cucinello, Stringer, and Swisher.

During the excitement of the bombing and bomb dodging, the *Pigeon* had somehow managed to rig Manila lines and tackles to her rudder. Later she repaired her rudder herself, using only the facilities she had aboard. The *Pigeon* was the same type of ship as the rest of us but she had been fitted out years ago as a submarine rescue vessel instead of a mine sweeper, and the repair equipment she had on board was valuable to all of us later on. For one thing, she kept the PT and the Q boats going. The only trouble with the *Pigeon* was that she had no regular antiaircraft guns; only machine guns. Being loaded down with submarine rescue devices, which were now useless since all but a few of our subs had departed the area long since, she had been thought too heavily loaded to carry guns. Dick remedied that.

When we saw him next morning, he had two beautiful three-inch guns. They weren't mates, but he was as happy as a kid with a new Christmas horn. One had come from the *Bittern* and one from a sunken sub no one had been able to rescue. Dick had to lift her tail out of the water before he could get at that gun, but he got it. And that wasn't all. They left the all-important splinter-protection shields—heavy steel plates to protect the gun crews—off the *Pigeon*. Some of the ships had plates that were too thin—

the *Tanager*, for instance. Thin plates let shrapnel in and it whirls around and kills ten men when it should kill one.

They had done right by the *Quail* as far as shields were concerned, and Dick wanted some too. Within three days he had dug down into the smoldering shambles and had dragged out the heavy plates necessary to outfit his ship and had welded them in place where they would do the most good. Before the war it had taken expert workmen to install our plates. Dick and his gang did their job in three days.

Small ships like ours work from a base or a tender ship. When we lost the Cavite yard we were homeless and felt like waifs. I've seen pictures of bombed families picking forlornly around in the ruins of their homes after an air attack. That is what we did all during the month of December. During the daytime we swept the channels through Manila Bay out past Corregidor to keep them clear for the few remaining subs and surface ships trying to escape from the area. But the nighttime was ours, and every chance we had we stole back to Cavite to poke in the ruins. When Cavite was first bombed the ammunition depot had caught fire. We expected to see it blow up during the night and kept a safe distance away from it. Through some freak of fate, the big fuel tanks were still intact also, though we expected to see them go up, too. Then in the morning, when we found nothing had happened, we got hungry for that oil. We had had pitifully little of it in our tanks during our yard overhaul and we wanted to fill up desperately. Just before dawn we eased the *Quail* alongside the oil dock and tied her up heading out, ready to break away in a hurry, in case of still another bombing.

Through the Indies

Morning brought no Jap planes, but we discovered that all the fuel-depot workmen had been evacuated. We merely broke the locks on the valves and ran down the oil ourselves. While we were filling our thirsty tanks we spied some Diesel oil in drums, and we rolled nearly sixty drums of it down and emptied it into our Diesel tanks. We carried a few more drums on deck and dropped them off later at Mariveles on Bataan. They were mighty important to us later on. Part of that oil helped carry us on our way to Australia.

Taylor cast a speculative eye on the ammunition depot while the engineers were busy fueling. We needed ammunition, too. The fires seemed to be only eating away the sides and the roof of the depot. The main portion of the place was made of stone blocks laid by the Spaniards many years ago. Still, an ammunition-depot fire is nothing to be casual about. Taylor stood and looked at it for a long time. Finally he turned to me and said, "I've got to do it."

I knew what he meant and let him go, sending a handful of men to help him. Maybe I shouldn't have, but if you've ever had a Jap bomber drop eggs on you while you gritted your teeth helplessly because you knew you had only a few rounds of ammunition left, you'll know how badly we wanted that ammunition.

In an hour or so Taylor came back wearing a broad grin and bringing with him a boatload of ammunition of every sort we needed. He'd walked calmly through a small fire and broken down the doors of the compartment to get at the ammunition, but he got it, which was the important thing. He'd also made another discovery. The fires were not serious so far as the ammunition itself was concerned.

The old Spanish masonry had been equal to modern bombs, and the fires had attacked only the framework on the outside of the walls. That meant we could get more ammunition and other ships could get more, too.

The Japs apparently didn't want to hit the oil tanks—probably thinking they'd get the oil themselves later. But we took care of that. All through the month of December we kept our tanks chock-a-block full of fuel.

In the depot there were stored some old naval three-inch broadside guns. As far as the Navy was concerned they were obsolete, but they looked as if they could still make growling noises in their throats, so the *Pigeon* carried them out to Mariveles.

Once we got them there, a couple of bright young Army officers spotted them, saw their possibilities as antitank guns, and mounted them on ordinary Army trucks. They could be trained and elevated, which meant they could be pointed like rifles, whereas ordinary Army fieldpieces cannot. Anyway, they did the trick. They broke the backbone of the Jap tank assaults in late January—months before Rommel used similar guns in Africa.

The *Houston* had left Manila before the war actually broke out. When she left, she left behind an obsolete and discarded 1.1-antiaircraft machine-gun mount. The *Quail* and the *Pigeon* both cast covetous eyes on it. It was too large for us to mount, and it finally went out to Corregidor, where the Army mounted it on the top of Malinta Hill. Old or not, it did a grand job there, and more than once chased away Nip dive bombers who were making it hot for the ships.

The Japs had a healthy respect for that old mount, and

it kept them from making effective dive-bombing attacks on the troops on Corregidor until late in April when they had knocked it out.

Manila and most of the island of Luzon were falling in December, and we were working against time to get as much useful material as possible out of Cavite and Manila and ferry it to Corregidor and Bataan. The crews of our small ships worked night and day during December. Deep down inside of us we had a good hunch as to what the future would bring, and when we passed Corregidor in our mine sweeping we eyed it and speculated on its strength and weaknesses.

Now it was late spring, and Corregidor and Cavite were around a corner of the past. We weren't in the middle of violent action any more but we were finding out that compared to constant wondering what the next minute would bring us and living in suspense, violent action was easier to take. Neck-deep in a battle, you move and act instinctively and don't have time to think and use your imagination. At least in a battle you could see and hear what you were up against and danger wasn't something unknown waiting to jump at you from behind the next coral island or clump of trees along the shore.

12

Engine Trouble

Now we were gathered around that chart on a tiny spit-kit of an island somewhere in the enormous area of the south Pacific. As Taylor put it, with simple eloquence, "Freedom is only a word until you have been close to losing it." Being free is like being immortal. And that's the way we felt.

We laid out our next hop to take advantage of the twenty-five-mile-wide shoal bank, extending down the coast of New Guinea. We planned to cross the Dampier Strait at night when there was no moon, for it was a well-frequented highway for Jap ships. We crossed it on the night of May 23.

Haley called me at four o'clock for my watch. It was very dark and cloudy. He said he thought we were making better time than we had counted on and were already opposite the wide gulf we'd expected to reach later that morning.

The island's mainland looked very strange indeed. Everything was hazy and indistinct. The sun came up that morning red and bloody. Over to the eastward we could

Engine Trouble

see the high mountains of New Guinea with an evil-looking overcast hanging around them. The whole coast had a forbidding aspect; the wind seemed as if it were blowing down from those mountains directly toward us. New Guinea, which is almost a continent in itself, is the place where all the weather in that area originated, born out of the air currents traveling up and down those peaks.

As soon as it became light enough, Binkley and I tried to establish our position. There seemed to be many more semisubmerged islands than the chart showed. The place was a navigator's nightmare. In all of that day's trip we hadn't sighted so much as a canoe. Finally toward late afternoon we spotted Pisang Island ahead of us. We had planned to stop there but, pushed along with the current, we were so far ahead of schedule we took advantage of the oncoming night to travel.

That night as we left Pisang, inky cloud banks rolled over us and the night was dark with gusty winds. Except for the increased roll and pitch, the hours were uneventful. When Taylor woke me to take my watch, the light in the hooded compass was very dim. I hoped it was a ground or a short in the wiring circuit, but I think I knew, even while I was hoping, that the battery was running down. I called Watkins, our electrician, and told him to give it the business.

He checked on all of the wiring and found the battery wasn't recharging. It meant an overhaul job at our next stop, but I knew if we stopped we wouldn't be able to start again. The engine had a generator attached to it, and Richardson and Watkins kept their fingers crossed and tried to get it to charge the battery.

"If it builds up, we'll be all right," they said, but they didn't say it with conviction in their voices. In the bleak and cold dawn, Binkley and I looked over to the islands ahead of us. We could just make them out. The more we looked the less they looked like the islands we expected to be headed for. This upset Binkley no end. He was sure that somehow we were a hundred miles farther along than we had thought, and were down by the Banda Island group. He was always worried about it if we weren't just where he thought we should be, because he dreaded having to explain our error to the boys.

"Let's figure it out logically," I said to him. "What we see over there looks like three islands. And one looks to be behind the other two. Let's look at the chart and see if there's a place with three islands grouped like that."

They checked perfectly.

Rubbing his hands gleefully Binkley announced to the crew, "I've got good news for you. We've been picked up by a favorable current and made twice our normal speed."

Everybody brightened up except Watkins, Richardson, and I. We had a dead battery on our hands the rest of them didn't know about.

By this time we had passed the Watubella group. Around eleven o'clock we arrived at Teoor, a good-sized native settlement. I had hoped to find a more sparsely inhabited island, but as we drew near and examined it with our glasses Steele said he spotted radio poles and antennae. We knew that these natives at best would be no better than neutral, and the thought that they might be able to send off a message about us made us turn north and head for a smaller island nine miles to the north. It was a low, flat, wave-battered bump of land. We figured it would be uninhabited, and it was.

"Guns, you take her in and anchor her," I said.

It was a rocky outcropping in the water with no beach, and since there was no beach we had to make a different kind of landing. Just offshore there were big boulders and beyond them deep water for fifty or sixty feet. We anchored from the stern, took a line over a rock, and tied ourselves up, leaving about six inches between the boulder and the boat to keep it from rubbing. Between the boulder and the beach were steppingstones of smaller boulders, but they were too far apart for us to jump from one to another of them and we had to wade, stepping on submerged coral-encrusted rocks. We tried it first barefooted, but it slashed and cut our feet and we gave it up. Before trying it again we went back to the boat and put our shoes on.

When all was secure Taylor told the engineer to stop the engine. No sooner had he done so than he made a frantic effort to pull the words back out of the air. He yelled, "No, wait." But it was too late. "I *would* be the damn fool that would gum the works," he moaned.

Richardson and I glanced at each other with only one thought between us. I made a motion to him with my thumb to push the starter button. He did. He pushed it once, twice, a third time. Nothing happened. Then he tore into the engine like a madman to see if he could find the trouble and get it started before it cooled.

Clarke and Newquist had taken a line over to the beach. They were sitting there half immersed in water, waiting for orders, but none came.

The horror of the thing gradually dawned on the rest of the crew. They crowded around Richardson, offering advice.

Meanwhile Richardson was going into the crankcase like a frantic mole, to get at the flywheel. There was no crank or manual means of starting the engine, but when he got it ripped apart enough to get a rope around the flywheel, so much of the engine had been removed it wouldn't have started anyhow.

The crew spouted optimism which they didn't feel but which they hoped would pep Richardson up. They said to him, "Boy, you just tell us what to do. Anything you want done we'll do it."

"That's fine," Richardson said, "that's just wonderful. The only trouble is I don't know what to do myself."

Taylor's only thought was to call himself all the blistering names he could think of. Watkins and Richardson were taking it hard. The engine, they felt, was their responsibility. It didn't make Richardson feel any better that only a couple of hours before I had said, "When we get to Australia we ought to build a monument for this guy Richardson."

But the others who knew nothing about engines refused to be downcast.

I had already put the engine out of my mind. I was positive that it would never run again. It might run for somebody else—not us.

The rest of the crew were accepting sail only as a last resort.

"I guess it's up to us," I said to Haley.

We were the only two who understood sail. Neither of

Engine Trouble

us liked the prospect very much. Our sail was clumsy. We'd never be able to beat up against the wind. Furthermore, the wind shifted around to the south southeast and began to blow in on us, and we were in danger of being blown up on the rocks. I called Newquist and Clarke back from the beach, told Haley to get busy on the rigging and step the mast, while I brought out the chart to see where we could go with sail. From the direction of the wind and taking into consideration our clumsy sailing rig I figured the very best we could do would be to reach Portuguese Timor, which was a dismal prospect because we knew the Japs had taken over that place. Our only alternative was to sail until we reached some small island and lay up there until we got a favorable wind. For all we knew, it might never shift. Our abundant supply of food didn't seem so abundant now.

By this time Richardson had got the crankcase back together again and the flywheel covered up. Wrapping a rope around a small coupling on the propeller shaft inside of the boat, he tied the other end of the line to a sturdy pole. Now following his directions, six or eight of the men took hold of the pole and tried to lift upward with it and spin the engine. This didn't work at all. The place around which the rope was wrapped was so small the woven hemp just slipped off, so Richardson sat down to think up a new one. It was getting on into the afternoon, and the wind the weather brought us was terrible.

Steele spoke up and said, "I see something coming and I don't like it."

Looking at the horizon to the northwest we saw the heads of about twenty men coming over the ocean's rim.

We watched them spellbound. Presently we saw the boat. It was a large war canoe. We had seen boats like it in the movies, but had never expected to see anything like it outside of a double feature. When they came closer we could see black faces painted with white streaks and bones stuck through the cartilage of their noses. In the rear of the boat, bending back and forth like the coxswain in a racing shell, was a much smaller man who might easily be a Jap, and this might be a local Jap patrol boat, manned by natives.

The boys all got down behind the mast barricade again with their guns pointed through loopholes. Head said, "Let me handle this, Captain. I'll talk 'em out of it somehow."

I wondered how he was going to talk them out of it if the little cox was a Jap.

Crouching behind the barricade, Cucinello had an idea. "If Head can talk 'em into coming alongside we can jump up and grab the Jap."

Each native had a spear laid across the canoe in front of him. We didn't know what the little guy in the stern had on his hip or under his armpit.

"O.K.," I said, "we'll let Head be decoy and you boys stand by ready to hop."

Head jumped up and made motions, beckoning them over to us. The coxswain gave an order, and they all stopped paddling. The boat drifted broadside to us and we saw then that the man in the stern was merely a shorter, stockier native, so I said to Head, "We don't want them now. Tell them to go home."

It was too late. They were already alongside.

The men stuck their heads up and gaped at these cannibals, and they gaped back at us. I told Swisher to try out his Dutch on them, but they couldn't understand a word. Head went to work with his international sign language to find out if there was any way of charging the battery in the town we had just skipped. He showed them the battery and pointed to Teoor. All they did was to shake their heads. Head changed his gestures.

"I am trying to get them to take me over to Teoor," he said. "If there's a radio station there, they must have some way of charging a battery."

"If you get into that boat with those head-hunters, you may never come back," I warned him.

He said it was our only chance. "All right," I told him, "but take Swisher with you and both of you take pistols and plenty of ammunition and don't let them sneak up behind you."

Head got into the stern of the war canoe and Swisher got into the bow so that they faced each other. The little coxswain started a chant with a regular cadence and the rowers all chanted back. Pretty soon they were out of sight. We felt pretty low about seeing them go. If we did have to fall back on sails we'd never be able to beat our way over to Teoor to pick them up. And they'd have to stay there.

It was getting dark and we turned in, feeling that after a rest we'd be better able to cope with things. Somebody got the bright idea of making cigarettes out of coffee, and the smokers among us tried it. It stank like low-grade opium. It was bitter and bit the tongue. You couldn't take it out of your mouth to complain about how terrible it was or it would go out. We wrapped it in strips of paper and smoked on it with the paper tubes tilted upward to our noses so that the coffee grains wouldn't roll out. It gave you an unhappy feeling in the guts, like the cigar you "borrowed" from your Uncle Joe and tried out behind the barn when you were a tadpole. But it had one benefit: none of us wanted to smoke anything for the next twenty-four hours.

At daybreak Richardson had a new idea: "If you deck hands can get this boat close enough to the beach, maybe I can get a line wrapped around the propeller and twist her tail that way. But you'll have to get us up in shallow water, no more than waist-high, so we can pull."

This particular cove had no sandy beach or bottom and was rocky and uneven underfoot. The keel started pounding the rocks and she banged the strut support running from her bottom to the rudder. With one man holding the stern just over a hole in the rocks, the rest of us got out into the water. Richardson put the middle of a long rope around the middle of the propeller, wrapping it cleverly so that the men pulling from both sides would spin it in the same way. In our opinion only a genius could have figured that out, so his stock went up again. We all got ready to pull. There were seven men on each end of the line. I stood behind the propeller and tried to twist it like a crank. I gave them a "Heave ho!" grabbed the propeller and gave it a turn, but the men on the lines slipped and fell in a choking, spluttering huddle into the water. A second and third attempt ended the same way. They couldn't get a foothold on the bottom. Richardson came over to help me turn the prop, but we couldn't budge it enough to count. It was in gear and if it had started we'd probably have been minus a hand or two.

Silently we got back into the boat and sat around and

looked at each other. We ate breakfast without having much relish for it and afterward saw a sailing banca bearing down on us from Teoor. I figured it was Head and Swisher coming back, or perhaps a messenger sent out to tell us that they had been thrown into the pot and fricasseed with dumplings.

Binkley started fumbling with the line and the coupling on the shaft.

"That won't work," Richardson said. "You're wasting your time."

Presently Weinmann got interested and went over to help Binkley. They were placing flat sticks torn from a packing case of sardines around the coupling, much as a first-aider puts splints on an arm, trying to build it up and provide a larger friction area. They gave it a try and when the strain came it didn't slip. It was solid. The rest of us crowded around now. We got out the hoisting pole with four men on each end of it. When they lifted, the engine turned over twice. Nothing happened, and some of the boys were discouraged, but I told them, "If you can turn over a Diesel at all, you'll warm it up by its own compression."

On the third spin it took off with a roar. It was the sweetest sound I had ever heard, bar none, and it was just in time. The wind had been piling it on during the night and we were rolling and pitching heavily. Just as we got the engine started, Head and Swisher arrived in the banca. They climbed aboard and began to tell their story.

"Save it," we said. "We'll hear it later. We've got to get away from these rocks, but fast!"

We lifted our anchor and got out of there. When we

reached the lee of Teoor, Head and Swisher got their chance to spill their yarn. They had almost become seasick in the war canoe, and the chanting business had got on their nerves. It was a long trip, but when they got there after dark they found one native who knew about five words of English and no Dutch. The radio antennae we had seen were the masts of a wrecked ship which the natives were using as flagpoles. No Japs had been there for three weeks. The natives were indifferent, but had said they would be willing to trade fruit and corn for anything we had and there was excellent water.

So we went on over and beached near the village. At nightfall we got under way again and tried to work our way against the wind so that if we had to run to port we'd have more room in which to run.

About three o'clock that night I woke up to find the bow riding up on top of the big waves and crashing down on them with a bang. I could feel the boards shudder with each crack. We kept on pounding along until about eight o'clock in the morning, we got in behind Keoor, a larger island than Teoor. In the lee of the island the sea flattened out. We approached the beach, casting a speculative eye on the native luggers anchored there. They were high in the bow and the stern and built like the boats used in the Middle Ages.

White flags went up along the beach and on the largest lugger, but as we coasted on down, looking for a channel into shore, the white flag on the lugger was hauled down and a Jap flag was hoisted. Looking through the glasses we could see that the men on her deck were all natives, and we figured there was a Jap captain hiding down below some-

Engine Trouble

where. The men brought out the guns, and keeping our barricaded side toward the lugger we eased in toward it. The Jap flag came down then, and we realized her crew was trying out all the flags they had, to make sure they showed the right one. Having run out of flags, they abandoned the lugger in a panic and rowed ashore, so we went on in. Head, Swisher, and Meeker went ashore to spy out the land. They talked to the natives and yelled back it was all right. Meeker came back to start our morning chow, and some of the men talked to the local schoolteacher, who had a school map of the area, and brought him over to me.

"The teacher can give us valuable information," they said.

My first question to him was, "What do you know about the Japs?"

He said he had a small receiver set run by batteries and had heard all the news on his radio and knew just where the Japs were. "Now they have all of New Guinea, all of the Solomon Islands, all of New Zealand, and all of Tasmania. They are fighting in southern Australia."

We made him verify it on his schoolbook map. He showed us where he thought the fighting was down by Melbourne.

"What language did you hear all of this news broadcast in?" we asked.

"Malay and English."

We knew that what he had heard was probably Japanese propaganda, but even though we told ourselves it was all a pack of lies it planted a worrisome seed of doubt as to what we would find when we arrived in Australia.

As I glanced at his map I noticed with horror a pencil

line running down from Corregidor and the Philippines right along the route we had taken, through the spot where we were now, and continuing on the route we intended to take. While our boys thought they were getting valuable information out of the schoolteacher he'd got enough out of them to stop our clocks.

I took the map, erased the pencil line, and told the gang to call off the morning meal and get into the boat.

"Now that we've given this monkey our telephone number and address, we've got to get going, sea or no sea," I told them. They were subdued and ashamed, and my anger gradually died away.

I could see whitecaps in the distance, and when we got past the point the wind came tearing at us, the waves bounced us around, and green ones came pouring over.

All afternoon we smashed our way through heavy seas until we reached an area of quiet water. A belt of coral heads barred us from the beach and we anchored about five hundred yards offshore to spend the night.

Richardson said he wanted to renew the stern tube bearing. It was made of hard rubber, but he had picked up a piece of lignum-vitae driftwood in the Jeff family group and had whittled out a new bearing for us in his spare time. We didn't question his decision, and, the decision made, it was up to Haley and me, as ship handlers, to get the boat up on a beach where the engineers could work on the propeller bearings. But first of all we had to wait out the dirty weather.

Morning brought a slight slackening of the wind and by noon we were ready to go. The sea was not too good but at least we could head directly into it. I struck up a song, and as bad as my singing was it had one virtue. You had to be a foot or two away from me to hear it. The howl of the wind and the throb of the engine took care of that. Occasionally some of the others joined in with me. I'm not religious and had no idea of being pious, but the first thing I sang was *Onward, Christian Soldiers.* Afterward I gave out with *Marching Through Georgia, Row, Row, Row Your Boat* and *Hail, Hail, the Gang's All Here.* I think that subconsciously I chose the songs that had the right rhythm for keeping time to the tiller swaying back and forth. Thereafter whenever the sea got nasty I tried to shout it down with off-key harmony.

What we saw when we drew near Taam was puzzling at first and then incredible. Time rolled back to the crusades, and a Mohammedan world with glistening mosques, minarets, and towers came over the horizon. Next the purple and maroon sails of dozens of good-sized vessels appeared. They had high, decked-over bows and sterns which went much further back in naval design than even the luggers we had just seen. Next the town itself swam up into view and, last of all, the people, wearing colorful costumes and the fez of the true believer. When we landed, contact close at hand with the inhabitants shattered our preconceived notions. They were noisy, diseased, and quarrelsome. They came out in small boats in droves, trying to poke their long-beaked noses into our business.

We let one or two of the leaders come aboard. They made motions like a salaam, bringing their hands down in front of their faces. We salaamed right back at them, but soon found out what they were doing wasn't a salaam at all. They were motioning us to go away. They pointed down at the boat, then off in the distance, and kept saying "Longeur," the name of a near-by island. But we were bent on fixing our bearing and ignored their invitation to leave. We explained to them in sign language we needed to fix the propeller and were going to take the boat into the beach, indicating we planned to do it tomorrow when the sun came up.

We had our dinner and turned in, sleeping with our guns at our sides to make sure they didn't sneak back on us and steal fillings from our teeth.

At nine o'clock that night the lookout reported a couple of boats coming out. In the boats were three or four old men, wearing flowing white beards and green fezes. We took them aboard and entertained them as best we could. The elders started a harangue about how elegant it would be if we'd scram out of there, and again we tried to explain to them that we had to beach the boat and fix it first. They pointed at the moon and jabbered. We didn't get it right away, but gradually they put over the idea they were referring to the effect of the moon on the tide. Meanwhile they discovered that Head was a doctor and made motions with their hands to indicate pains in their stomachs. Head gave them some cough medicine with a strong dash of codeine in it, hoping to put them to sleep.

He explained to us what he was doing, and we sat there waiting for them to drop off so we could go to sleep ourselves, but apparently they were immune. The only effect the stuff had upon them was to make them ask for quantities of it to take ashore for their friends.

About eleven o'clock their motions became even more violent, and it was apparent they wanted us to get in through the channel while we had high water and get the job over with rather than wait for high tide the next day.

We made it plain to them if they wanted us to go in the night they'd have to provide a pilot for us. It was quite a feat to get it over to them. But by this time Head had worked up an almost miraculous system of gestures and motions to take the place of words. He jerked his head violently up and down for "Yes," using the motion either as a question or a statement, and did the same thing for "No," by shaking his chin from side to side until I thought he'd shake it loose from its moorings. He'd point at a place or thing and express eagerness to be there or to leave it behind: he'd register joy or anger or disgust with supercharged pantomime, and before he'd been at it long he had the person he was trying to sell thoughts to doing the same thing. It was tedious and it took patience and perseverance, but he stuck at it. I still can't believe he came up with some of the information he came up with, or put the thoughts in his own mind into the minds of others that I saw him do, but by God he did it, and that was all we cared about. He would have been hot stuff in the early days of the silent movies when you couldn't mug and overact too much for the audience.

They supplied a pilot, but we didn't trust him too much and took soundings ourselves all along the way in with poles.

Apparently nobody in the town ever slept. They came crowding around us impertinent, curious, and noisy. One of them, apparently a Mohammedan priest, insisted that Head and myself sleep in his home. Taylor escaped because he had dozed off while we were entertaining them.

The priest's home was close to the beach, and we made arrangements with our lookouts to come in and check on us every once in a while to see if our throats were cut.

We tried to sleep on a straw mat, but they didn't let us sleep very much. The room was full of wild-eyed gents, talking at the top of their voices. They must have called in all the green-fez men on the island and they paraded around us while we lay there, explaining how the green-fez wearers had made the trip to Mecca, using words like Java, Singapore, and Mecca to put over the idea of a long journey. After the green-fezes went away, Taylor and I got about an hour's sleep.

We woke up about four o'clock in the morning to find the boys in the boat in a turmoil.

"For God's sake, Captain, can't we get away from these A-rabs?" they begged.

We found out that the boys out in the boat hadn't slept a wink. The swarms of townspeople climbing aboard to peer into the sugar can or the earthenware rice crock almost drove Meeker nuts. They picked up every article on the boat, and had to be watched like hawks to keep them from stripping us bare. About every half-hour Meeker would rush along the deck, swinging a meat cleaver in big circles to shoo them away.

By this time we were as anxious to go as the Arabs were to have us leave, so we got out in the waist-deep water and replaced the bearing. We finished the job about five o'clock but had to wait for the next high water at eleven. Meeker was too upset to produce any breakfast. We couldn't even have light snacks, for no sooner did we pick up a banana than three long noses would be closer to the banana than ours.

Long before high water, we started pushing the boat along the bottom, trying to get as far away from the place as possible. As we left they went into paroxysms of delight, laughing, howling, waving their arms, and jumping up and down like whirling dervishes. Just for the hell of it we pretended we were coming back, and their faces dropped a mile.

Dutchmen we met later told us that the place was the religious center for all Mohammedans in that part of the world, including the Moros back in the Philippines. They also told us that if we had been a smaller outfit and hadn't been heavily armed our precautions about throat cutting would have been necessary.

13

The Last Lap

THE GALE had still not howled itself out, but if we started direct for Australia and ran with the wind we'd miss the continent entirely and never be able to make a landfall. We wanted to cover as much distance to eastward as possible while we still had the shelter of the Dutch East Indies and we figured that by quartering across the troughs of the waves instead of riding straight over them we could just about make it. So we headed as much into the wind as we possibly could. As soon as we got outside of the shelter of the island of Taam, the weather was blustery and the seas ran high.

This was our worst night at sea. Things went fairly well until six o'clock. Dark clouds had been piling up in the east for several hours and at six they slapped us in the face with blinding rain. The wind kept shifting from southeast to the northeast and then back to southeast again. Try as he would, Taylor couldn't keep the boat from batting hell out of its bottom on the waves. Cross-waves hit us and rolled big green ones over the engine cockpit, but by slowing down the engine and being careful with the tiller we managed to keep the boat from pounding her brains out.

After my watch was ended I held onto it instead of calling Haley to do his trick. It was impossible to see anything with the wind ripping the crests off the high rollers and throwing them into our faces. The rain came in squalls lasting about fifteen minutes each and while it lasted it was like standing in a shower bath—not a shower in a private home with a modest little spray squirting through the few holes left unrusted, but a locker-room type of shower from which the jets burst in almost solid water. During the rain squalls the waves smoothed out and up would go our hopes for calmer weather, but after the squalls the wind howled again and the waves built up, higher and higher, until we were taking green ones aboard with a thud and the crew went back to their bailing.

It kept up without letup until around ten o'clock, when I'd had enough of trying to buck it alone and called Haley. I stayed with him on the tiller and we changed our course to the northeast, intending to run into the lee of Longeur even if we didn't land there. The boys were bending over, scooping up water in their bailing tins, slinging it overside, then bending again for more. The bilges were gurgling and the green ones were leaking through the decking, but I managed to find a spot where we could examine the chart by flashlight without having it soaked and checked off the distance we'd made since Taam. We'd gone too far along to make Longeur, so there was nothing for it but to run with the sea and lose all of that valuable distance to eastward we'd been piling up for the last week. I set a course for the northernmost island of the Tanimbar group and went back to give Haley the new course.

I was simply and honestly scared out of my wits. I had been scared ever since we left Taam. Once when I had been stationed in Panama I had had a boat sink under me in waves just like the ones we were playing leapfrog with, and every time a green one came aboard I lived through that Panama affair all over again. The Panama boat I had been on was a submarine wherry. I was supposed to go ashore in it with another man and blow up an Army observation post with phony dynamite during a war game. We came up to the beach just as the tide changed and a big roller hit us. The wave didn't go over our heads but I could feel it break over the boat, and the boat was gone. I was sitting there rowing when all of a sudden right in the middle of bringing my oars against my chest I wasn't sitting in a boat any more and the oars were rapping me on the chin. The next moment we were swimming.

Now Haley and I discussed how we'd get our bow around through the trough and complete the swing to get the wind and the waves on our stern. Haley figured that trying to do it would finish us.

"I'm game to try it," he said, "but we'll never make it—never in *this* world."

I didn't like the emphasis he gave the word "this." The crew didn't know anything about small boats. Haley and I were the only ones who knew what the sea could do when it had the bit in its teeth. The men back in the engine pit were wide open to the elements and every wave that went over us filled their nostrils and throats, strangling them. We were lucky we had a Diesel. No gas motor could have stood that perpetual ducking. A gas job would have shorted and sputtered and quit, leaving us to be tossed around from

The Last Lap

wave to wave like a football in a game of keep-away. But our Diesel ran just as well under water as above. The compass light had been grounded out and we had to use a flashlight to see it from time to time.

We stood there waiting for a low one in which we could turn. Meantime we cursed the cross-chop waves. You don't notice cross waves unless you're in a small boat. A small boat like ours could go up one wave and down another as long as there were steady, even swells. Even when the long ones break you can give them the slip by nudging your tiller at the right moment and not taking them head on. If you did the trick correctly the boat rolled right over the white-maned ones like a rocking chair on a slight bias. But while we were doing that the cross-chops hit us with nasty, jarring slap-slaps that came aboard even when they weren't big enough to rate coming aboard.

Haley and I picked out a good one, swung her hard over, and then we were in the trough between hills of black glass cradling us for the kill. We speeded up the engine; she answered the tiller like a lady and we were still afloat. But we weren't out of the woods yet. We had both heard about waves catching up with you from behind and rolling over you from stern to bow and we waited for that to happen, but gradually it dawned on us that it wasn't going to happen to us. Whether there was something special about the way our stern was built or whether the whole thing was just an old salt's tale based on sound, fury, and grog we never knew. We didn't care, so long as it wasn't true in our case.

We weren't taking any green ones now and the crew bailed all of the water out and went back to sleep. I made up my mind that the next island we came to we'd hide behind for six months if need be, until the sea let up or the wind changed. I'd had a bellyful and Haley had, too. I looked down at the others sleeping there in a wet, tired, unconcerned pile, and envied them. As long as the boat floated that was all they cared about. They were spared the wear and tear of knowing what *could* happen, with a mistake of a fraction of an inch in handling the tiller or hitting a wave a hand's breadth the wrong way.

In the morning we saw the island of Moloe where we had expected to see it. As soon as we got in the lee of the island there was a remarkable change. It was as if we had passed through a curtain and on one side of that curtain a gale was howling and on the other side was a calm, peaceful, tranquil tropical paradise where birds sang and butterflies fluttered. It wasn't the first time we had gone through such a curtain, but once more it made the men feel that the gale had blown itself out. They never seemed to get it through their heads that a lee shore was merely a pocket of calm in a hurtling, angry world.

We cruised leisurely down the coast. The water was very clear. We could see the white bottom a hundred feet down and the cliffs came right down to the water's edge. It reminded us of Hawaii. We saw several good camp spots but we would have had to wait for high water to get near them. About a mile north of a native village we found a place we could get into without too long a wait. We hoped the natives wouldn't come up to visit us, although it was hoping against hope because in the cove there was a grove of coconut trees and we had found that natives and coconuts were never very far apart from each other.

The Last Lap

We anchored stern out with our bow up on the beach, tied to a tree. To our great joy we found at one end of the beach a little mountain stream coming down, splashing and tinkling and falling into a place that would do for our private swimming pool. Standing under it gave us a private shower. A little higher up was a place we could get drinking water. We sent Doc Head up to examine the water, and he reported that it dropped down straight from the mountaintop.

We'd been there for about an hour when a few natives in a small boat paddled in and sat down on the beach about forty feet away from us. We didn't speak to them or pay any attention to them, remembering the last natives we had seen, who got into our hair like nits and almost drove us crazy. But these natives turned out to be all right. Seeing us gathering wood, they pitched in and gathered it for us. We were clearing a place for a camp and they helped us do that. They watched us trying to crack coconuts for a while, then took them away from us and gravely showed us how to do it properly, and all without our speaking to them or having them make the first move to break the silence.

Finally we broke down and said, "Good morning." Once the conversational barrier had fallen, we found that they spoke about twenty words of English.

Since Australia was so near, Binkley got to work on an American flag with a needle and thread he found in Head's miracle bag. He began with a white oblong made of bits of white skivies all sewed together and worked on that as a base. He cut up blue dungarees for the blue field and ran up against a stone wall when it came to the red stripes—but not for long. Reaching into Head's bag once more he pulled out a bottle of merthiolate, a red antiseptic fluid, which he used as a dye. We left him alone to do his Betsy Ross stuff undisturbed. We could see that, like any creative artist badgered with questions and bothered with kibitzers breathing down his neck while he was composing a masterpiece, he was likely to boil over at any moment.

After he was done we inspected his handiwork. He had taken a short cut to get his stars. Rather than cut them out and sew them on (which would have taken days), he had made holes through the blue material in the shape of stars and allowed the white to show through. Somewhere along the way he found that if he made the stars a decent size he wouldn't have room to get them on, and, having made up his mind he'd have big ones or none at all, he had compromised on twenty-four instead of the conventional forty-eight. The number didn't bother us. We thought it was a swell flag, even when we discovered it was strictly a one-way flag. The reverse side was a blank. He eyed us defiantly and explained that if we held it up in the direction we wanted it to be seen from and didn't let anybody get behind it no one would know the difference.

The natives brought us a little raw tobacco and one pack of Dutch cigarettes. We tried making smokes out of raw tobacco wrapped in paper. They knocked our heads off. But they weren't as bad as the coffee cigarettes we had tried.

The place was beautiful at night, too. Maybe it seemed beautiful to us because it was our last night of camping out together. We had about three hundred and sixty miles to go and if we got fair weather that meant about three days'

The Last Lap

running time. We couldn't believe that Australia was so near.

After dark we sat around the fire, talking. One of the things we remembered were the two one-legged officers back in the Navy tunnel—an Army air officer and a marine. They were two of the most cheerful people in that dusty hole. They had lost opposite legs and they walked around arm in arm like a two-headed, four-armed giant. When they drew shoes they drew one pair for both.

Another thing we talked about was the Navy dentist in that same tunnel who with very little to work with had made whole sets of teeth for those who had had theirs shot away. "Remember how those guys with toothaches used to sit around and worry about how much he was going to hurt them?" Wolslegel said. "They wouldn't think as much about a five-hundred-pound bomb dropping on them."

Then we got to talking about the Oscars we had got (not the Hollywood kind) and how the *Quail* had earned a reputation as a bird dog.

Early January had brought a short rest for us mine sweepers. Manila had fallen. We'd moved to Corregidor and done all that seemed humanly possible to establish a new base of supplies and make repairs at the Rock and at Mariveles. Corregidor was being bombed every day and the *Quail* was being bombed along with it. Still, we got a little sleep at night and after a while we began feeling restless again. We decided that Corregidor was taking too much from the air. On their good days it was averaging one Jap plane down out of every six formations that came over, but that wasn't enough. We'd had more experience by this time and we weren't afraid of high, flat bombers attacking us as long as we were out in the open bay where we could maneuver. We figured that if we steamed out well away from Corregidor and placed ourselves directly in the line of attack of an oncoming bomber we could get in some good licks on them before they reached Corregidor's main fire power. That way we hoped to spoil their aim at the Rock and break up the strength of their attacks. But it didn't work out as we had planned. We did get one sure "heavy" and one "probable" (they were usually too high for our guns), but we didn't break down their bombing morale. Once a Jap bomber goes in for his attack nothing stops him unless he is shot down. But we did give Corregidor warning of a new wave of attacking planes.

We noticed another thing about the Japs. If they were after a certain target they made no effort to attack a ship which happened to be able to make things hot for them. Maybe the next day they'd come back and try to get the offending ship, but not at the time. Finding this out gave us an idea and gave the *Quail* its "bird dog" nickname.

During January it was the mine sweepers' routine to take night-patrol stations north and east of Corregidor close to the south shore of Bataan. We were supposed to be watchdogs for Corregidor and see to it that no enemy landing boats sneaked up on the Rock at night. This turned out to be pretty dull stuff, since the Philippine Q boats (similar to our PT boats but smaller and less seaworthy) patrolled farther than we did out in the bay and nothing ever got by them. They were fighting terrors and loved nothing better than chasing Jap armored barges, and as a result such barges were getting scarcer each night.

The Last Lap

At daybreak, whichever mine sweeper happened to be on duty went back to South Harbor. Corregidor could see for itself by day and the ships only obstructed their arc of gunfire. About nine o'clock in the morning the Jap heavies started working and we piled out of South Harbor and went into our daily dodging tap dance. We noticed that at about seven o'clock each morning the Japs sent over an observation plane which circled around Corregidor at a safe distance but at a fairly low altitude to get a better look and do a preliminary sizing-up job. This plane got on our nerves. First we called him the Colonel, figuring there was a brass-hat Jap in it. Later we called him Oscar. But the more the "sweep" skippers thought about him, the more we were convinced that he was our meat. He usually came over when we were coming back from our night-patrol stations. But his flying route was almost exactly over those stations. Most mornings there were broken clouds around Corregidor and Bataan, and it was Oscar's habit to dip down through a hole in the clouds, take a good look, and then zoom back up until he came to another hole in the clouds, where he ducked through again. We decided to cure him of this habit.

With our sweeps strung out on our night stations we dallied for a while before returning to South Harbor and worked our way under likely-looking breaks in the clouds. The first time we tried it we got the best results. The *Quail* nailed him on his first break-through. He flipped over as though he were looking at us indignantly and staggered off, wobbling like a drunk. Before he could get back in the clouds the next sweep gave him another burst and finally way down the line near Mariveles the *Tanager* finished him off, and he plowed into the side of Mariveles Mountain. I don't think his headquarters ever knew what hit him, for we got quite a few other Oscars before they learned to fly high and keep out of harm's way.

When Oscar retired to higher altitudes, our lives went back to always dodging and never dishing it out. Over on Bataan our four or five lone P-40's made occasional dawn attacks on Jap airfields. This seemed to annoy the Japs a lot, and they started dive-bombing and strafing our airfield at Cab Cabin on Bataan every morning about seven o'clock. The *Quail*'s night station was close to the airfield, and we watched this operation helpless and futile as we were returning to South Harbor.

They circled high in groups of nine and then came down in Indian file over the top and down the slopes of Mariveles Mountain, swooped low over the field, and pulled out over a row of trees which fringed the shore of Manila Bay.

The antiaircraft guns on the field had two strikes on them because Jap planes coming down the slopes were protected from A.A. headaches except for the few seconds it took them to pass over the field. But we figured that if we worked our way in close to the shore and behind that fringe of trees, the Nips would run right into our fire on their pull-out. We had to use our fifty-caliber M.G.'s for the job, as it was too close range for our three-inchers. Fifties aren't ideal for that work. They could wing a plane, but the winged planes don't fall right away and sometimes could get back to their base. Larger-caliber machine guns would have been better, but we didn't have them. Even so, we did pretty well. We brought three of the Japs plunging into the bay, and there were two probables.

The Last Lap

We didn't look for any trouble from other Jap planes that morning but we figured the next morning they'd be on our tail for a little revenge. Only the next day we weren't at the Bataan airfield at seven o'clock. Instead we sneaked back to South Harbor early to get under the protection of Corregidor's 1.1-inch old faithful. The first Jap that came down into South Harbor was literally smothered with steel and flaming tracers. No more Japs came down that morning.

We waited for a couple of days at the airfield and caught them again, but they didn't come after us in South Harbor any more. What they did do was a whole lot more embarrassing to us. They started to hop our Philippine Q boats. The Q boats were game and brought down three Japs of their own, but we felt we had got them into it, so we went steaming up the bay to help them out and that finished our bird-dogging, for we were very late in getting back to South Harbor and had to explain to our boss where we'd been and why we were late. Our division commander and the commander of inshore patrol pretended to be annoyed with us for our bird-dogging, but they didn't put much conviction in the bawling out and I guess they weren't too much put out about it.

Thinking about our "bird-dogging" days and falling Oscars made us feel better. It was pleasant to think of a time when we had been standing toe to toe with the Nips, lifting a swift one from our shoelaces and bringing it home with a thud on their ugly chops. It made the business of ducking and dodging and twisting through strange waters for our lives easier to take.

In the late forenoon of June 1, the clouds stopped scurrying over the rim of the mountain. There was only blue sky and a bright sun. The men wanted to be on their way, but we had to wait a little longer for the seas to calm down. I promised them if the good weather continued we could leave on the night high tide. There wasn't much work to do that day. We cleaned up the boat and stowed our gear to prepare for more rough weather if we ran into it. The sun set red. That old gag about a red sun at night meaning fair weather didn't have much meaning in those latitudes. For all we knew, the weather might never get better than medium good in that Arafura Sea, and we started to call it the Our-Fury-Sea.

We didn't believe what the native schoolteacher told us about the Japs having a toehold in Australia, but there might be an element of truth in it and we had to be prepared. Bercier suggested that the Japs might be bombing Darwin when we arrived, but we guessed that a few more bombs wouldn't make any difference and we weren't going to let them interfere with our plans. Steele was all for waging an eighteen-man war on the Japs if we found them in Darwin, and he and Cucinello worked out a plan for chasing them across the desert from the rear. The idea back of their campaign was that while the Nips were advancing southward across the Great Australian Desert to meet our own Army in the south of Australia, we would come down on them from the north and cut off their supply trains. One of the weaknesses of this brilliant strategy was the fact that we didn't know whether the United Nations had an army in southern Australia or not.

We were completely out of touch with the world and didn't know what to expect. The men were deathly afraid

The Last Lap

we'd get orders to surrender ourselves to the Japs when we arrived. They thought that maybe someone in authority would tell us to surrender because General Wainwright had ordered all Fil-American troops everywhere to lay down their arms. Our guess was that the General had been confronted by a threat of death for his men unless he said what the Japs told him to say. The Japs had no military right to ask for more than the surrender of the troops in the area which they took over. But being Japs they asked for Corregidor when Bataan collapsed and they asked for all of the Philippines when Corregidor fell. By their own admission in the Jap-controlled Manila newspapers we had seen at our second stop, they had threatened to continue the slaughter of the unarmed troops on Corregidor unless all the Philippines surrendered.

That night we rehashed every minute of the past five months. We'd gone over each one of them a hundred times before. Some of the men, like Cucinello, had had temporary duty on Bataan, and bit by bit we had pieced together the complete fabric of those months so that in our own minds we felt we knew what had happened and why. We sifted the conflicting stories and compared them with what we had actually seen from our own ship where we had had a grandstand view of both Corregidor and Bataan. We ruled out such stories as the one about Corregidor not having shot down any Jap planes because its guns couldn't reach that high. We were in the business of winging Jap planes ourselves and we knew that there were times when Corregidor averaged one plane out of every six that flew over it as long as it had guns and ammunition to do it with. A lot of officers in the tunnels never believed those Jap planes were falling. With their limited opportunities for observation they couldn't see them brought down. When they did get a look they were apt to see them fly off apparently unhurt and not see them in the distance when they nose-dived into a mountain or the bay.

Then we talked about what part of Australia we wanted to reach first and we decided that the point closest to us was the first point we wanted to hit. Our chart showed us that would be Melville Island, just north of Darwin. We made up our minds that if, when we got there, we found that the Japs had taken over the place, we wouldn't give ourselves up. We would seize a boat bigger than ours, one we could go across the Pacific in, if we had to.

The food and drink we were going to load up on in Australia loomed big in our talk. Newquist was going to go to a soda fountain and order a double row of sodas, then a row of milk shakes, fancy ones with complicated names. When he polished them off he was going after the ice-cream supply. Newquist was the lone teetotaler among us. The rest of us were about evenly divided between a steak as thick as an encyclopedia and a barrel of beer. One, who shall be nameless here, was going to get him a girl to love him before he even thought about steak or beer.

We stayed up all that night until high water and at two-thirty we took the boat out. We cruised along in the lee of Moloe Island in calm water until five o'clock and when we reached its south end and turned east we still had protection from the lee of Yamdena Island. Around noon the next day we passed through a narrow channel between Yamdena and Vordate and were in the open sea and rough water again. Not dangerously rough—the kind of roughness that breeds wet misery arriving aboard in the form of heavy spray. The boat still slapped her floor boards on the waves but not so hard that we didn't think she could take it.

The weather held blowy and rough until about sundown, then calmed slightly during the night.

On June 3 we had to throttle down to keep the floor boards from smashing against the waves, but the gang refused to be downhearted about it. They could almost smell Australia. About midnight I woke to the realization that we weren't rolling and pounding so much and called back to ask Taylor to give the engine all she'd take. In the forenoon it was calm enough for us to change our course open up wide and drive straight toward our goal. It was the first time we had done it in an open sea and we felt like a PT boat. At two o'clock we hoisted our one-way flag, and the boys were standing up shielding their eyes with their hands, competing for the first sight of land.

On the dot of four o'clock we made out what looked like a pencil line on the horizon. It was low and even but unmistakable. With the binoculars the men swore they could see water tanks, but as we came closer the tanks turned out to be trees and hills. About two miles away, we saw forbidding chalk cliffs, sheer and dropping straight down three or four hundred feet to the water. They were crowned with a black streak of topsoil near the top. There wasn't a sign of human habitation anywhere, just a blank, eerie bleakness. We coasted along looking for a break in the cliffs which would be one end of Melville Island, or better still the Apsley Strait, which ran between Melville and Bathurst Islands. There were several deep indentations, but they looked alike from the sea and we couldn't tell whether they were blind alleys or openings going all the way through. At sunset we picked out one at random and headed toward it. Binkley and I looked at each other and smiled. Our thousand-to-one shot had panned out. The water was muddy instead of being clear as it would have been if the passage had merely been a bay or inlet.

The place was laid out on a tremendous scale. Even in the mouth of the strait we could barely make out land to the west, but we got well in and anchored for the night.

In the morning we started up the strait.

Binkley and I knew we couldn't be anywhere else, but the men began to wonder if we really were in Australia after all and gave us the old razz-ma-tazz, asking us whether we had brought them to New Zealand or even Africa. We went up that passage for an hour. Finally we rounded a corner and saw several long, one-story buildings made out of planks. We headed for a little cove, beached the boat, and a group of very black, tall, bearded men, painted all the colors of the rainbow, came down to meet us. They were knobby and misshapen. Some of them had hair colored a violent red and scrubby beards colored white.

Before we tried talking to them, a white man with a long black beard cut square across the bottom, and wearing a pair of khaki shorts, walked down the path from the hill. When he came close enough I yelled, "Hello, there," and a twanging voice came back, "Hello there, Yoonks." It sounded more like that than "Yanks," but it's impossible to reproduce Australian vocal sound effects even with trick spelling.

"What place is this?" we asked.

The Last Lap

"It's Melville Island, Australia," he replied. "Don't you know it?"

Binkley grinned from ear to ear. Miraculously our navigation had hit the jackpot, homemade sextant, no current books and all.

"Where do you hail from?" black beard asked.

"Corregidor," we told him.

"You had quite a trip of it, didn't you?"

"Yeah, quite a little trip," we agreed.

We asked him how the war was going. "The Japs came over here a while back, but your Kittyhawks chased them and knocked them all down," he told us.

We had our gear ready now and went ashore. The man we had been having our jabber with was Brother John, who with another monk named Father O'Connor ran a Jesuit mission there.

We stayed at that Jesuit mission from nine in the morning until three the next afternoon. It was our first chance to sleep in real beds for as long as we could remember, but we couldn't get used to it. We rolled and tossed in the unaccustomed softness and finally got up and prowled around restlessly until dawn. Father O'Connor was chagrined and felt that his accommodations weren't good enough for us. We tried to explain that they were *too* good, but he merely looked baffled.

In the afternoon we went down to another mission at the other end of the strait. We left there about midnight and arrived at Darwin on the morning of June 6. When we crawled out of our boat, the Aussies grabbed us and took us into their inquisition room for questioning, figuring we looked like suspicious characters. I don't blame them. I had a look at a mirror and I was a double for Haile Selassie. The rest of the gang were no prettier.

Even when they were satisfied we weren't the seagoing half of Coxey's Army, we were still in a hell of a fix because there wasn't any hotel or rooming house in town where we could stay. Just when it began to seem we had come two thousand miles for the privilege of standing forlorn and alone in a street, Colonel Wortsmith of the U. S. Army Air Corps took us under his wing, guided us to his headquarters, gave us a place to sleep, and gathered odds and ends of clothes for us from the scanty stock he had. Some of his men gave us shirts and shorts. They were tropical-weight garments, but as far as we were concerned no expensive tailor could have turned out such luxurious duds.

Two days later the Navy sent an Army transport plane for us. We piled into it early in the morning and flew all day. That night we hit Adelaide, squatting on the plane's bare metal seats. It was colder than a penguin's undercarriage in that crate. It may have been summer where we'd come from but it was winter down under. After a night in Adelaide we took off for Melbourne. We arrived in Melbourne looking pretty disreputable with our legs and knees bare. I was lucky enough to bump into an Annapolis classmate who took charge of us and got rooms in a hotel. The hotel had no heat in its rooms and we were just about frozen, so at dinnertime we all boiled down to the dining room bent on food and warmth.

The place was run on the American plan and the menu offered three major dinners. One built around steak, a second with roast chicken as its main prop, and the third depended on mutton. With each one of these dinners there were about twenty other items; three or four soups, a dozen vegetables, olives, pickles, and two or three kinds of desserts. When the waitress asked, "What will you boys have?" we said, "We'll have what's here on the paper."

She put her hands on her hips and looked at us fish-eyed. "Listen," she said, "I don't mind lugging the stuff in here if you're going to eat it all, and not leave half of it for me to take back to the kitchen."

Her voice was no dulcet purr. It boomed all over the room, and the rest of the diners stopped eating to look at us. We told her, "You bring it out, sister, and leave the rest to us." She brought it out and we ate it. Newquist topped off his chicken and fixin's with three different kinds of ice cream.

When we were through she said, "I never thought you'd do it. You must be fair famished."

We let our belts out a notch and said, "How about the other dinners? We've had the chicken; now we want the steak." She went away looking wild, and we saw her discussing the thing with the woman who ran the place. The news worked its way back to the chef, and he put his head through the kitchen door to share the excitement.

When she came back she said, "You can have them, but we'll have to close up the place and not let anyone else in because it will scrape the bottom of our larder."

The nameless one among us who wanted a girl to love him more than steak or beer when he reached Australia got his girl. As a matter of fact, he got a whole bevy of girls, until the problem of keeping them untangled and out of his hair threatened to be more of an ordeal than any we had gone through in our thirty-one-day trek. And the funny part of it all was, of all the crew he would have been the last one I would have guessed had Casanova blood. I hadn't had much of a chance to see that side of the gang doing its stuff.

A week afterward the news came that thirteen of us were to be sent back to Sydney for active duty. The night before they left, Head told me the boys wanted to get together for a farewell dinner.

We went in together and sat down. All except Head, who stood back of his chair, holding something in his hand. He began to make a speech. He said, "I've been designated . . ." but that was as far as he got. His voice tightened up and he held his hand out to me. "Take it," he said.

They had chipped in and bought me a watch. On the inside of its case were engraved the words, TO OUR GALLANT SKIPPER FROM SEVENTEEN GRATEFUL MEN.

I stood up and tried to make a speech myself but I was as bad as Head. So I said, "Well, you know how I feel about it," and quit. It seemed to be enough.

There was one more present. They had remembered the crack I made about how if we ever got to Australia we ought to build Richardson a statue. It wasn't a statue; it was a suitcase. Then having got all of that off our minds, we sat down and ate.

Two days after the dinner party, Cucinello, Stringer, Taylor, and I were sent to Brisbane by plane and hopped the Army transport *Tasker H. Bliss* (since sunk off Africa) for home.

Forty days later we were in Key West. The *Bliss* car-

The Last Lap

ried a load of Aussie student aviators and one Aussie nurse. She was a prim little wench but she taught us how to wash and iron our clothes in salt water, which is something no one should have to learn ever. You can't get salt water to make suds and when you're through washing your clothes they're stiff as boards. Six pounds of starch wouldn't put more iron into them.

From Key West we took a bus to Miami.

When we got back to Miami everything seemed marvelously neat and clean and unperturbed and calm and rational.

Taylor and I were hurrying to get back to an air-conditioned restaurant in our hotel and cool off. We cut across a street jaywalking, and when we glanced up, there stepping off the curb and coming toward us was a Jap. We stopped and stood there. We could feel our hair tingle like a dog's ruff bristling. Things whizzed through our minds so fast they were just a blur. The Jap didn't pay any attention to us and sauntered by.

We were both silent for a few moments, then I said to Taylor, "Well, we got through that. It's happened now, and I guess we'll be all right from now on."

We kept on toward the restaurant. Taylor said, "I'm glad it was us instead of Steele and Cucinello and the boys. They might not have been able to make it."

But I'm not worrying about them. After what they went through, they can take anything.

Right now I've been assigned to a ship readying for action on any one of many fronts. The drumming guns of Bataan and the bright bloody hell of Corregidor are far away and behind in the past. There is nothing those of us who were there could wish for more than to go back and tear down the prison gates of Fortune Island. However, others may be given the privilege, and perhaps not all of us will be there when we haul the red-balled flag down from over Corregidor.

But all the rest of my life I'll be waking up at night, seeing a dock flaming like a funeral pyre as we pull away from it, or a couple of Filipino mess boys handing me a roll of pesos, or I'll be in a thirty-six-foot boat caught in a current between two Jap patrol boats.

Maybe after a long time these things will grow dim, almost as if they never happened. But I doubt it. I think they'll get clearer and more sharply defined. As clear and sharp as the engraving on the back of a watch I'm going to give to my son when he grows up.

EPILOGUE

I'm writing this on the day after Christmas, 1942. The crew of our Diesel boat is scattered as only a global war can scatter men. Meeker is on a destroyer at sea. It was hit by bombs, but Meeker is O.K.

Bercier, Newquist, and Clarke are at a mine depot in Australia. Mines were their specialty and it was natural for them to end up in such a berth.

No one knows where Watkins is. I have written to the others but have drawn a blank.

Weinmann is back in Honolulu.

Richardson is on a destroyer in the Pacific.

Cucinello is at the Naval Training Station at Sampson, New York.

Swisher is on a new cruiser being built on the East Coast.

Steele had to swim ashore from a destroyer sunk in the southwest Pacific, but he made it.

Stringer is now on a submarine at the sub base in New London.

Taylor is a naval aviation pilot with the rank of Ensign at Pensacola.

Haley and Rankin had to swim ashore with Steele when his destroyer was sunk in action.

Wolslegel is on a destroyer tender and hopes to get married to an Aussie girl.

Binkley is the only one of the seventeen reported missing or killed in action. Head was on the ship with Binkley and was badly burned. He is now at the San Diego Naval Hospital.

All of the seventeen were promoted one grade in rank. And all of the members of the scuttling party, Taylor, Weinmann, Steele, Cucinello, and Meeker, got the Navy's Silver Star.

Most of this information I have picked up out of letters I have received from the seventeen from time to time. One from Meeker, dated September 24, at sea, is a good example.

> September 24, 1942
> U.S.S. *Blank*
> At Sea

DEAR CAPTAIN:

This is a short letter to let you know that ALL of us are thinking of you. I guess all of us wish that we could be back there with you serving on the same ship. As far as I know we are all still alive and growling.

Pat Haley, Steele, and Rankin are Refugees again. Got mixed up with a torpedo but made out O.K. Saw them before I left. They seem to think that they are going back to the States this time for sure. I hope they make it. Wolslegel is about to get married if he can get permission. So I guess he wants to stay here for the duration. The girl is a pretty nice kid and a swell cook. I eat up there every time I get a chance to horn in.

I am in excess on here and they gave me the oil-king job plus the compartments. It's a good racket but it doesn't seem to get me any closer to home. By the way IT was a girl on that last keel laying. I owe you a cigar.

The folks back home don't realize how tough this war is or how much it's going to take to win. This ship has had a couple of tough days since I have been on her. We got credit for two or three planes and a sub all within twenty-four hours. Seemed like old home week for a while. We were hit lightly and lost a few men. We are operating now and doing all right.

It's time to knock off now. Won't be able to write anything else without disclosing military secrets. So long and drop a post card if you get a chance.

              Chief cook and bottle washer,
                          J. F. MEEKER

A NOTE ABOUT THE AUTHORS

John Morrill was born in Miller, South Dakota, and reared in Minneapolis. He was graduated from the Naval Academy in the class of '24. His first loves were submarines, but in June, 1939, he was transferred to the mine sweeper Quail *as commanding officer. His specialty is navigation and he is now navigating officer of a new cruiser. Since writing this book he has been made a full Commander. His nickname is "Shug" (short for sugar), a tag fastened upon him at the Academy.*

Among his prized possessions are a bowl, spoon, and pipe made for him by friendly Filipino natives who sheltered him during his voyage of escape. With his wife he shares ownership of a cocker spaniel, Chloe, who saw history being made. Chloe was at Pearl Harbor when it was bombed, together with Morrill's family.

He and the other seventeen men who ran the Jap gantlet with him hope to get together for a reunion party after the war. All that are left of them.

The other half of the writing team of Morrill and Martin was born in Charlottesville, Virginia, and attended the

University of Pennsylvania. After having been thrown for a loss by three months in the University hospital he made up his own curriculum, taking such courses as Italian, history of architecture, outdoor sketching, and all the English and history he could get. He also ran on the track team, edited or was on the staff of three campus publications.

He has worked in a logging camp, as a stevedore, as back-shot man for a survey party, and has spent two vacations riding across country from Detroit to California helping deliver cars from factory to dealers. He says it is his idea of fun. He's an over-the-road-trucking addict and wrote a Saturday Evening Post serial about the men who drive them. He has also written or collaborated upon about twenty short stories and forty or more articles which have appeared in the Post, Cosmopolitan, Vanity Fair, American, The Ladies' Home Journal.

He was art editor of the Post *until the early part of last year, when he became a staff writer with the title of associate editor. He is married to Virginia Bird Martin and they have two children, Peter, 13, and Margery, 10.*

www.ingramcontent.com/pod-product-compliance
Lightning Source LLC
Chambersburg PA
CBHW080333170426
43194CB00014B/2553